The Face in the Mirror

The Face in the Mirror
Teenagers and Adoption

Marrion Crook

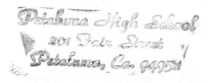

ARSENAL PULP PRESS
Vancouver

ARSENAL PULP PRESS
103 - 1014 Homer Street
Vancouver, B.C.
Canada V6B 2W9
www.arsenalpulp.com

The publisher gratefully acknowledges the support
of the Canada Council of the Arts and the B.C.
Arts Council for its publishing program, and the
Department of Canadian Heritage through the
Book Publishing Industry Development Program
for its publishing activities.

Edited for the press by Linda Field
Typeset by Robert Ballantyne
Cover photograph provided by Tony Stone Images
Printed and bound in Canada

CANADIAN CATALOGUING IN PUBLICATION DATA
Crook, Marion, 1941-
The face in the mirror

ISBN 155152-079-6

1. Adoption. 2. Adoptees-Identification. I. Title.
HV875.C76 2000   362.73'4   C00-910249-3

Contents

Acknowledgements

MY THANKS GO FIRST TO THE OVER FIFTY young people who gave me their time and their information. I agreed not to publish their names and so cannot thank them individually. Thanks also to the Adoptive Families Association of B.C. who, with the Chris Spencer Foundation, supported the more recent research project.

Following is a list of people who offered suggestions and information when I first began researching. Some are quoted in the book and some are not. All added greatly to my knowledge, and I appreciate their interest and their caring attitude toward the teenagers I was trying to understand:

Mary Beauchamp, Program Officer, Department of Social Services, Government of the North West Territories; Child Welfare League of America, New York; Susan Drysdale, Co-ordinator, Children in Care, Department of Social Services, Halifax, N.S.; Pam Hendy, Canadian Adoptee Reform Association, Williams Lake, B.C.; Anne Lea, Adoption Resource Centre, Edmonton; Dolores Lindsay, mother of five, Winnipeg; Clair Marcus, author, adoptee reform activist; Joyce Masselink, Social Worker, Ministry of Human Resources, Victoria, B.C.; Linda MacDonald, Canadian Adoptee Reform Association; Nancy Nelson, Community Worker, Victoria; Patricia O'Brian, Ministry of Community and Social Services, Toronto; Irene Patterson, Program Consultant for Adoption Exchanges, Fredericton, N.B.; Rolland Perrin, psychiatric social worker, Department of Health, Williams Lake, B.C.; Wanda Pillon, Parent Finders, Victoria, B.C.; David Ross, Friendship Centre, Williams Lake, B.C.; Audrey Scrammell, Canadian Adoption Reunion Registry, Victoria, B.C.; Mark

Spence-Vinger, Department of Human Resources, Williams Lake, B.C.; Betty Stinston, Social Worker, Department of Health and Human Resources, Whitehorse, Yukon; birth mothers, Anna K., Kelli A., Tammi K., Barb H., Lou S., and Chris P., who gave me hours of their time. I am also grateful to the many parents and adopted adults who phoned and visited with their stories in the hope that they would help others.

Special thanks, too, to the ten teenagers who agreed to share their time to help with further research, and others, in particular Dièdre and Danielle, who kept calling to encourage me, and Karen Madeiros, Helen Mark, Margaret Robinson, Anne Melcombe, Jennifer Hillman, Margaret Kwong, and Harriet Sancott, all of the Adoptive Families Association of B.C.; Rodney Louie, Stliatliimx, Band Chief; Gail Barth, Jennifer Murn, and Fern Crook, adoptive mothers; Danielle Finnegan, an adopted adult who read and commented on my manuscript; Lizabeth Hall, Scott Clark, and Mark Handley, United Native Nations; Betty Stewart, Parent Finders; Joss Halverson, Librarian; Sharon Jinkerson, aboriginal adoption counsellor; Vivienne Green and Christine Patsey of the Gitanmaax Reserve; Dean Fortin, adopted adult who read the manuscript; and the many people who have taken the time to tell me their adoption stories. You are all, in some way, a part of this book.

To all my children with gratitude
for all the lessons they have taught me.

Preface

IMAGINE HUMAN LIFE as a gigantic tapestry. We weave our own lives into that fabric—our ideas, feelings, and plans, slipping them around and through the plans and ideas of others and into our family patterns that expand and become more complex as we add and blend in threads from other sources.

This book was written for adopted teenagers who, like all teenagers, are entwined in their family patterns and in the larger fabric of the social world. It is written as well for the parents, teachers, counsellors, social workers, nurses, doctors, and friends who surround them. Adopted teens have something different from their friends in other family circles—a loose thread that may need attention before they feel complete. Some tape this loose connection to themselves and try to ignore it. Others trace it back to its origin and leave it there. Still others carry a long disconnected burden that entangles all the relationships of their lives.

The patterns are often not simple ones. It was this emerging view of the complexity of being adopted that set me on the path of research and discovery with teens.

I read books to my children about adoption, but by the time they reached twelve, I couldn't find any in my city library or book store that spoke to teenagers. My sons, both adopted as infants, never asked me about their backgrounds, and I wondered what they were thinking. They answered my questions about adoption with a brief "yes" or "no," and a kind of bland indifference. Didn't they care? Did any teenager care? Did anyone know what teenagers thought about adoption? My curiosity grew, as did my concern that I might need to know more, that a lack of books and information might be hiding something important. I decided to find other adopted teenagers and ask them: "What do you think about being adopted? What do you know? How do you feel?"

I borrowed every book on the subject in my local library. Using a friend's computer, I did a search on all books in print on teenagers and adoption, and using another friend's university card I raided the college library. I read every book I could get my hands on that had anything to do with the subject.

In the summer of 1985 I packed my Dodge van, bribed my twelve-year-old son David to come with me, and headed south from Williams Lake. My friend Nancy, who was seven months pregnant, her eighteen-month-old son Max, and Felicity, the twelve-year-old daughter of a Winnipeg friend joined us in Vancouver. From there the caravan went east, gypsy-like, along the Trans-Canada Highway with Max's play-pen strapped to the roof-rack. We stayed with friends and relatives along the way. I interviewed adopted teenagers who were daughters, cousins, or friends of my friends. In this casual and random fashion we wandered over the prairies and arrived in Winnipeg where Delores, a busy mother of five with no time to look for adopted teenagers to interview, had put an ad in two city newspapers asking interested teens to call her number. And call they did. Her phone rang for days. I crouched in the pantry, the only quiet room, writing down teens' names, ages, addresses, and detailed directions to their houses. For four days I drove around the city listening, taping, asking them questions.

In the fall I stayed in Vancouver, put an ad in the city paper, and collected names and addresses that kept me interviewing for six weeks. I also did some interviews with friends' children, and friends of friends' children in my then home-town of Williams Lake, B.C.

This sample of teens was random. I couldn't control how many were eighteen, or how many were girls and how many boys (22 girls and 18 boys), so I can't say that the results of my interviews are an accurate and typical reflection of the whole population of teenagers. I tried to get as varied a response as possible, but I certainly wasn't rigid about it. With one exception, all the teens I interviewed had been placed for adoption as infants, so I did not report on the difference between those who were adopted as infants and those who were adopted as toddlers or older children. Some researchers, such as Victor Groza and Karen F. Rosenberg (1996), do show distinctions based on placement age, but I did not interview enough teens adopted at an older age to do so. I didn't do any interviews with teens who were not adopted, so I relied on the research and writings of others to note differences between the adopted teens I interviewed and those who were not adopted. With these few restrictions, I listened to, recorded, and transcribed the fascinating stories of the teens.

When I started the interviews I was afraid that I wouldn't find out anything at all, that no one was at all concerned about being adopted. My own two boys had lulled me into thinking that the circumstances of their birth were of academic interest only. In fact my oldest son, eighteen at the time, said, "What are you doing a book on adoption for? No one's going to buy it. Nobody cares." He was wrong. The teens surprised him and they surprised me. I had suspected that there was some dissatisfaction, but I truly wasn't prepared to have teens so *passionate* about the whole concept of adoption. I asked them to teach me about what it's like to be adopted, and they certainly did.

I resolutely ignored my own experience with adoption and my sons' indifference, and imagined any number of questions teens might want answered. What did they see as their needs: to know about birth parents? To know about their medical history? To know what kind of a family their birth mother came from and what kind of work she did or does? Whether their father was a lawyer? A logger? A drunk? Did they have trouble with the idea of adoption only if they didn't get along with their adoptive parents, or did they have trouble with the idea even when the relationship was good? What did they want to know about themselves? I asked these questions and the teens told me much more than I could have imagined. The names have been changed and sometimes descriptions are altered a little to protect their privacy, but the quotes are accurate.

I published the findings of this research and then found that with new laws, new attitudes, and a faster exchange of information, the world of adoption began to change very quickly. As my children grew, as I read more and listened to more stories of others, I learned how notions of adoption were changing in our society and in the lives of teens.

In the fall of 1997 I attended a conference on aboriginal adoption and realized from the material available that no one had investigated and written about how the teens of today were reacting to the new world of adoption. One of the organizers at the conference asked me when I was going to do more studies; there were new questions to investigate. Why wasn't I looking at these questions, he wanted to know. What was it like to have two sets of parents? Did the adopted teens feel more secure or more threatened? What about those alarming statistics that claimed that a significant number of jail inmates were adopted, that a significant number of disruptive children in school were adopted?

My own adopted boys were now adults, the oldest a husband and father of two boys and not at all interested in finding his birth family—so he said. My youngest son had connected to his birth mother and aboriginal family, heritage, and community. Change was happening in society, and in my own life.

In an interview for a sports story, I suddenly stopped my questions, looked at the man I was interviewing and said, "I think you're my oldest son's uncle." We discussed my son's birth and found that this man might be the brother of my oldest son's biological father. (After checking, we found that he wasn't, but he knew my son's paternal birth family.) It seemed eerie that, in a city of two million, I should interview someone who knew my son's birth father.

The tapestry of life weaves around us sometimes without a great deal of planning on our part. With this serendipitous meeting, I felt as if I had been entwined into someone else's story and given new threads to follow. My children now have new connections, threads which may weave around and into their tapetries. Slowly my children may begin to look at themselves as part of a bigger world and become involved in a more complicated set of relationships.

What is that widening family circle like for teens? Do they find this relationship web comfortable? Suffocating? Threatening? Reassuring? What do they think would be best for them?

By this time I had two computers, my own Internet link, and five library cards. I had written fifteen books since I first wrote about adoption and had more contacts and research skills, but the expert source of knowledge on adoption was still the teens, so I needed to talk to them. I asked the Chris Spencer Foundation for help. They were enthusiastically supportive and voted to finance more research. The Adoptive Parents Association of B.C. were also encouraging, and offered to manage the funds and give me referrals to teens. This happened so quickly that it felt as if I were suddenly carried along by a project that had an energy and life of its own.

I found teens who had been adopted at birth and were now dealing with adoption, and others with an obvious racial difference between themselves and their adoptive parents. I talked to ten, four boys and six girls, in this phase of the research. I also talked to four birth mothers who had given up a child years before, a birth father who had suddenly found a teenaged son whom he had not known about, a father who was searching for his child, a single woman who had looked for and adopted a child racially different from herself, and four adults who had been interviewed for the original book when they were teens. The world of adoption—being adopted, adopting children, giving up a child—is a dynamic and changing one full of diverse personalities and people with strong opinions.

The teens I interviewed in this phase of the research talked to me about culture, prejudice, belonging, and grounding in ways that would have seemed very sophisticated years ago. The teens were knowledgeable and often thoughtful. The differences between the teens today and those of the first phase of the research are not differences in the way they feel about adoption so much as in the number of relatives and relationships they must deal with in their families. As well, teens today are more used to doing research—a skill that's now taught in schools. There are many search sites on the Internet which don't require any registration or fees so teens can easily access them. Has increased information about birth parents led to a more secure feeling in teens? Does increased knowledge bring with it different problems and different fears? Is there counselling available on the subject of adoption? Do we have a sense of the usual process of development for adopted children, or do we still believe that adopted children do not have particular development issues? My interviews with the teens showed that they had many of the same feelings and ideas that teens had in the past: feelings of loss, a need for knowledge of the past, fears of rejection, and concerns about hurting adoptive parents.

The questionnaire used in the interviews was designed to explore the teens' views of many aspects of adoption. I wanted to have some way of comparing their answers and making sure that I covered all the important subjects. One of my temptations when interviewing is to become so interested in what is being said that I get off the subject completely. The questionnaire was a way to make sure that I talked about adoption and not the mileage on my car or the latest movie. As well, I met the teens in private so that they could expand on the questions and say as much as they liked. A spirit of inquiry was established so that they clearly understood that what they told me might become part of a book that would be useful to others. They were also assured that their identities would be disguised.

I taped their stories and listened to them over and over. Having written eight novels I didn't anticipate any problems writing. What I hadn't realized was that fifty personalities were clamouring to be heard and expecting me to make their opinions clear to others. It took a lot of sorting, searching through tapes, thinking, and re-checking what the teens had said before I could start. My responsibility was to tell others *exactly* how those teens felt, what they had said, what they had meant. I looked for common themes and also any exceptions as well as using, in many cases, one teen's words to tell a common story.

The teens I interviewed came from Canadian cities—Vancouver, Calgary, Winnipeg—and from towns and rural areas as remote as northern British Columbia. They lived in many family constellations—one brother, two sisters, no siblings, four brothers—had loving families and abusive families, wealthy families and middle-income families. Some of them had left home and were supporting themselves; others still lived at home. They were white, black, and aboriginal, with degrees and variations of colour. They ranged in age from thirteen to twenty-two and all were adopted. Their personalities were as different as their complexions. Some were curious and helpful. Others were passionately anxious to tell others what they had gone through and how they saw the problems of their age. I interviewed them in beautiful homes where Inuit carvings sat under exquisite paintings, and in dark apartments where roommates and boyfriends hung over the backs of the chairs listening and adding comments. I interviewed them in my car, in restaurants, in shopping malls, and in many homes.

I expected to find the teens polite and a little distant, since I was, after all, somebody's mother, so I was pleased and grateful that they were so frank and willing to talk. I was continually surprised at how much adoption mattered to them. Their feelings couldn't be contained in short answers to a few questions. My own prejudices and ideas were swept away in their explanations, conversations, and the talking, talking, talking they did about adoption. The research became a long conversation with fifty teens about their feelings and ideas. Sometimes they told me quietly, sometimes emphatically; but they wanted to tell me and, through me, the rest of the world what it was like to be adopted. I became a vehicle for their expression and this book became theirs.

The ongoing story of adoption continues to grow, including more and more affected people. Grandparents, aunts, and cousins have relationships which, in the past, have been ignored. Tribal affiliations, ethnic heritage, family medical histories, and genetic information have come to be increasingly important as we as a society learn more about ourselves. An adopted child comes with connections, and it is those connections that he or she is looking for.

"Mom," my son said on the phone after the first week of his move to his aboriginal territory and his birth family, "everyone is a cousin!" It may be that the discovery of "all our relations" where "relations" includes our ancestors is much more complicated, rich, and important than we had previously believed.

Introduction

BEFORE EUROPEAN CONTACT and continually since, the Native peoples of the North American continent practiced adoption. They decided among themselves which children should be raised in families different from their biological families. This customary or traditional adoption, one without legal papers, is still practiced in some communities, particularly where property is communal, so inheritance doesn't depend on wills and legal divisions.

On a visit to Arctic Bay, Nunuvik, Canada, I listened to my teenaged friend, guide, and interpreter as she pointed to a busy, twelve-year-old neighbour. "that's my cousin. Actually he's my brother, but he was adopted as a baby by my aunt and uncle." Customary adoption here seemed simple, co-operative, frank, and useful. There was no secrecy about the children's origins and all the children knew where they belonged.

This is in stark contrast to adoption in southern urban centres where lawyers, welfare agencies, and medical staff are involved in adoption, and where adopting parents seldom know the birth parents. How did we establish such a different view of adoption?

Prior to the 20th Century
The practice of sending children to families other than their family of origin probably occurred in the society of early Britons as it did in aboriginal society, but organized adoption as an institutionalized social movement is documented as far back as 1618 in English history when orphans were sent to Richmond, Virginia. Over the following 350 years, 150,000 children were transported by boat to the colonies. The last orphan boatload left Britain for Australia in 1967. Many of the

19

children sent out to the colonies were not adopted into a family in any sense, but were used as labour. Children did not have rights and the abuse of children was not generally considered to be a social offence. Christian brothers in Australia tortured their orphans, and farmers in Canada treated girls like slaves and beat them. No one took any responsibility for the sexual, physical, and emotional abuse of those thousands of children. Anyone—parents, teachers, neighbours, instructors, religious leaders, employers—beat children without legal or social consequences. Not all the children who were sent out were abused, but few were adopted as a member of a family. People had large families, sometimes twelve children, many of whom died in infancy or early childhood. Society did not invest much in a child who may not live to adulthood—children were not considered valuable social assets in the white North American population. In some families they were loved, perhaps, but not legally important. Adoption in these early years among the white population was not common. In any case there were, in the British legal system of North America, no adoption laws. You could register a non-biological child as chattel, but you could not adopt.

A new look at children came with the writings of Swiss-born Jean Jacques Rousseau. In spite of his personal failure as a parent—he placed all five of his infant children in foundling homes where the death rate was so high that survival was unlikely—he wrote a book that influenced the way society viewed children. In *Emile* (1760), Rousseau proposed the unusual idea that humans were born "good" and, if carefully educated, a child would be joyful, productive, and moral. This was at odds with the prevalent attitude that children were born bad, full of evil and sin, and needed to be disciplined in order to become "human." As well, Rousseau contributed to the romantic notion that children in their innocence could be examples to adults and be of benefit to humanity. While this does not seem a very startling idea today, it was revolutionary in Rousseau's time. Rousseau's writings were read worldwide and his ideas gained a hold on the popular imagination so that, in time, children began to be viewed as valuable in themselves. This changed attitude influenced official policies.

Still, in spite of changing attitudes, the treatment of children didn't improve a great deal. Bad educators and parents still routinely caned children. Children worked in unsafe conditions for long hours.

They were poorly fed and neglected. Charles Dickens, writing in the 19th century, did not report great philanthropic movements to rescue children. But the romantic notion that children were "jewels" and "precious angels" contributed to some improvement in the coming years. People may have continued to abuse and neglect children, but society was beginning to view this as not the fault of the children, and to feel some responsibility for rescuing them.

Capitalizing on this attitude during the middle of the 19th century, Marie Rye and Annie McPherson organized homes for British orphans in Canada. Playing upon the public image of philanthropy, Rye and McPherson successfully ran a child-transportation business that moved children from Britain to Canada, promising better opportunities for them and, incidentally, netting the two women a profit of 100 percent. This with the full approval of both the British and Canadian governments. When an inspector from the British government investigated their business in 1874, he found that the children were often mistreated. Collective public attitudes of philanthropy and care were countered by individual tolerance of child abuse and maltreatment. Between 1870 and 1925, approximately twenty-five organizations were sending children to Canada.

Charles Loring Brace, a Protestant minister, was not in the business of transporting children in order to make himself a fortune. He was truly philanthropic, although certainly misguided. He helped to establish the Children's Aid Society of New York to improve life for children of the poor. Between 1854 and 1929, the Children's Aid Society moved over 100,000 children, called orphans but often not orphans, from the streets of New York City to homes across the U.S. Some of the children were adopted as members of a family, but many were used as child labour. At this time most children were still not seen as valuable for their potential contributions to society, but for there contributions to farm life. The question was not whether to adopt, but how much work they could perform. Few were adopted.

In England, adoption was not legal until the 20th century because social class was inherited and only blood children had a right to their class. To adopt a child from a lower class meant risking all the problems of the lower class, a view that has persisted with surprising tenacity to the present time. "Bad blood"—the blood of the poor— seemed to carry moral faults. In the U.S. and Canada, the notion of class was of much lesser importance. The American ideal promoted the concept that an adopted child had as much chance of "becoming President" as any child. Brace and the Children's Aid Society saw themselves as philanthropists serving the great democratic ideal of equality, giving abandoned and orphaned children new homes across America, and new hopes. In reality, those children were often picked off the trains like slaves at an auction, used and abused by their "foster parents," and suffered greatly. The Society did not advocate legal adoption, because most of the children were not legally orphans, and the only form of legal adoption at the time was the process of registering the child as a possession.

1900-1940

By 1929, most states in the U.S. had enacted adoption laws that gave children some protection, and, at least, established that they were indeed orphans before they could be placed.

Canada's most famous orphan was fictitious. Anne of Green Gables was an orphan in Prince Edward Island in the early 19th century. The attitudes of the community and her foster family at her arrival to the home were typical of the time. She had been chosen to work on the farm. The foster parents, particularly Marilla, felt virtuous and practical when they asked the orphanage for a strong boy, but, after originally planning to send her back, decided to keep her. Fortunately for the reading public and for the story, love was much more important than labour.

The purpose of adoption laws during the early part of the century was not simply to allow for the disposing of family property—the right of adopted children to inherit and the right of adoptive parents to bequeath property to their adopted children—but also to provide the child a good home. Rousseau's notion of the essential goodness of the child had by now replaced the ideas that a child is born wicked, and that the children of the poor are born more wicked than most. In view of this changed attitude, every child deserved a good home. Agencies recognized by the courts were set up to match children to "good" homes. The notion that children needed protection, and that the legal system needed to ensure they were placed in a home where they could be well-cared for, evolved in the early 1920s and has been part of the adoption placement system with greater and lesser effectiveness since.

Infant formula was discovered in the 1920s, making early adoption much more possible. Until then the adoption of infants was not practical unless the family could afford a wet nurse. After the invention of formula, infants could be placed into a family at birth, and the family could pretend that the child was born to them. And so the substitute child, "as if born to," arrived in the family and the secrecy around the birth of an adopted child began.

Before this, there was little importance placed on secrecy. By the 1930s and '40s, the identification of birth parents and adoptive parents was screened by bureaucracy. The original notion of privacy and confidentiality around adoption served the idea that the child should be protected from being branded illegitimate—a social stigma that was real and disenfranchising at the time. As well, the confidentiality laws protected adoptive parents from being harassed or blackmailed by unscrupulous birth parents. Because of a few, all birth parents were blocked from knowing where their children were placed. Psychologists, social workers, and others involved with the children believed that it was in the best interests of the child and adoptive parents to deny their child's birth parents, family, and situation in order to create a new life for the child. An amazing amount of hubris, including a belief in the superiority of the adoptive family, went into this attitude.

1940-1960

The years of the Second World War and those immediately following saw many more babies available for adoption. Brief encounters and the desperate intimacy of the war years produced many babies without families to care for them.

During the 1950s, while an increasing number of babies were being placed for adoption, Jean Paton wrote a book, *The Adopted Break Silence*, in which she related her own experience and propounded the notion that adopted children should know who their birth parents are. She established a reunion organization called Orphan Voyage and began the movement that advocated the right of adopted children to find their biological families. This movement had slow beginnings. Her point of view had to wait twenty years before the increasing numbers of adopted children placed in the '50s reached adulthood and could embrace her ideas.

The 1950s were a time of great change in adoption. As well as many more babies being placed and more social acceptance in the mainstream culture of adoption, changes occurred in the placement of non-white babies. Children who were not white had experienced great difficulty in being legally adopted. The continued customary adoption in aboriginal groups and within the black communities of the U.S. was not recognized by law, but certainly it was recognized by families. At this time agencies began to make efforts to place non-white babies. The 1950s and '60s brought a concerted and organized effort by both U.S. and Canadian adoption agencies to increase the number of placements of aboriginal and other children of colour with white families. This occurred at a time when there were fewer and fewer white babies available for adoption. It was also a time of the Civil Rights Marches in the U.S., with the public becoming more and more aware of the dangers of racial prejudice and the necessity of opening hearts and minds to interracial acceptance. So, with practical and altruistic motives, the "Big Scoop" of Native children began.

When the issues of poverty, social prejudice, and disenfranchisement resulted in difficult lives for the children of the poor, particularly the poor of the many reserves and reservations of North America, the social agencies' response, in retrospect, appears appalling. They ignored the customary adoption processes of the communities, rounded up the children and, like the orphan trains of the 19th century, displaced these children by the car-load or bus-load from their home communities to adoptive or foster homes across the country and into other countries. Britain received plane loads of aboriginal children from Canada in the 1950s, and many aboriginal children were taken from Canada between 1958 and 1967 by the Indian Adoption Project of the Bureau of Indian Affairs and the Child Welfare League of America in the U.S. The parents of these children were often coerced or assumed to be uncaring, and at times the children were stolen, that is, taken when the parent was sick in hospital or away gathering supplies. There are many stories of social workers taking the children "for now, while you are sick" and never returning them. This was part of an inexplicable assumption of the superiority of the white race, and given that astounding belief, children were assumed to be better able to have a good life away from their families. Unstated in this "Big Scoop" was the notion of genocide, the assimilation of aboriginal people into the white society and their eventual disappearance. Not all adoptions of aboriginal children at this time took place under these circumstances. Some birth mothers voluntarily placed their children in non-aboriginal families and do so today, but many did not sign consents, or were coerced or tricked into signing consents.

The residential schools of the time, which thousands of aboriginal adults had attended, left many incapable of parenting. The residential schools, with the same motivations of assimilation and even genocide, had robbed them of the experience of being a child in a family home. When they grew up and had children, parenting was difficult. Instead of addressing this need to learn to parent, social agencies removed their children. It has taken thirty years to reveal the extent of this problem, and the consequences are likely to challenge generations to come.

Prior to the 1950s, black children were not placed in white homes, but by 1967 there was a concerted effort by adoption agencies to change this. In the 1960s, agencies advertised to white families through religious organizations and public appeals to adopt interracially. These were successful in increasing the number of adoptions of Asian, black, and aboriginal children, but primarily into the homes of white families. In British Columbia between 1961 and 1971, agencies placed many more aboriginal children in non-aboriginal homes than they had before. This was alarming to the aboriginal communities and, in 1972, in response to pressure from aboriginal communities and organizations, the provincial government put a moratorium on the adoption of aboriginal children by non-aboriginal families. They feared another "Big Scoop." This moratorium stayed in effect for three years.

In the U.S., increasing demands for Indian homes for Indian children were being made by the Adoption Resource Exchange of North America at the same time that adoption agencies were sending aboriginal children out of the area and out of the country. In 1979, 339 children, many of whom were aboriginal, were sent from Canada to the U.S. for adoption, because aboriginal children could move across the border without legal hindrance. This situation was both astounding and horrifying to First Nations and Native American groups. Most aboriginal communities in the U.S. and Canada are clusters of family constellations that have endured for centuries. Every child has a place and is valued as a member of a family cluster. Adopting the child out does not change this. The child is valued simply because he or she is a member of a family. The child belongs. Losing the children, especially in such great numbers, caused emotional pain and horror and created huge problems for family reunification and tribal affiliations. In an effort to reverse this drain of children away from their home communities, aboriginal associations demanded Indian homes for Indian children.

In 1972, representatives of black communities in the U.S., the National Association of Black Social Workers, objected to the placing of black children in white homes for much the same reasons as the aboriginal people had. They cited problems of psychological adjustment for these children, believing that such a placement resulted in difficulties in establishing a personal and secure identity. The children would not know who they were.

As a consequence of these efforts by representative organizations, agencies now try to place children in a family of their own race. However, children are still placed trans-racially. This does not mean that such racially different homes are second-rate homes, but it does mean that parents in these placements now are more aware of the importance of race. Parents today realize that race plays an important part in a child's life, particularly during the teen and adult years, and that they must not deny this difference and must address it directly. Parents are far less likely today to ignore the impact of race on their child than they have been in the past.

1970-present
By the 1970s, the number of babies available for adoption had been reduced, substantially due, among other reasons, to increasingly effective birth control, legalization of abortion, reduction of the stigma of illegitimacy, and the infertility of couples who were waiting longer to have children. The attitude toward adoption moved from placing children in order to meet the needs of adopting families, to selecting families to meet the needs of the adoptable children. When the scarcity of adoptable children emerged in the mid-'70s, families who wanted to adopt included couples who were infertile, couples who were fertile but chose to adopt, those who already had biological children, single men and women, lesbian and gay singles and couples—a greater diversity of adoptable families, or a greater frankness about that diversity. These families began to look across national borders for children. They now

considered children of other races and "special" children, those with physical and psychological needs, as suitable. These were the same children who had a decade before been considered unadoptable.

The fantasy of the "matched" family began to fracture when adoptive parents searched for and accepted trans-racial children into their homes. Families now looked different, not just in hair colour and physical features, but also in skin colour. Such an obvious difference advertised "adoption," and families began to find the notion of secrecy somewhat absurd.

With this new attitude toward frankness within the family, parents were advised to tell their children very early that they had been adopted. With this information children would not feel, when they discovered the fact, that they had been lied to. The lie was considered to be more detrimental to the child's mental health than the fact of adoption. The changing social attitude toward greater acceptance of adoption, and the increasing frankness within families about it, made adoption a more obvious part of society.

As the children who had been adopted in the age of secrecy (the '40s, '50s, and early '60s) grew up, they began to protest the former secrecy and to organize advocacy groups to agitate for their right to know their heritage. In response, institutions—not without protests and counter organizations from threatened adoptive parents—began to make changes in law to accommodate the demands of adopted adult children. Established in Britain before moving into North America, the changes in legislation gradually made finding birth parents more and more possible. The need to know one's biological roots began to seem legitimate, especially when it was expressed by adopted adults who had very strong ties with their adoptive families and who appeared to have rational reasons for searching. Looking for birth families became a goal not only for the abused, the disturbed and the unstable; it became a legitimate and common need.

The "need to know" became the "right to know" and developed into the notion of Open Adoption, which meant that all parties—the birth parents, adoptive parents, and children—could know each other. So we circle back to the ways of our ancestors where children were placed in homes that had the ability to care for them, and everyone knew where the children were.

Not everyone wants this, and, at this time, there is a combination of Open Adoption, confidential adoption, and passive adoption, where interested parties can request information and other interested parties can permit or refuse contact. There is now more choice at the time of adoption and both birth parents and adoptive parents can consider more options for their child.

From the early days in North America, when aboriginal people accepted children into families as valued and equal members on the witness of other tribal members, we moved to registering children as legal members of a family with legal rights while we devalued and often hid the child's heritage. From the attitude that the child was a possession that was given up by one set of parents and owned by another, we moved to a view that the child has two sets of parents—the biological and the nurturing/legal parents. Today's views of adoption may include the concept that two sets of co-operating parents provide the child with a secure environment. Legal conditions need to be in place to protect the child, but as readers encounter the teens in this book, they will see that it is not always clear what the protection should be, or what connections should be maintained. We learn as we grow and now understand that the needs of adopted children are unique and must be considered, so that we no longer disenfranchise children from their right to a sense of belonging in society. It is my hope that the teens who speak in this book will encourage an adoption process that includes their views.

Chapter One

Placement

LIFE DOES NOT BEGIN AT PLACEMENT. For too long parents and adopted children have talked about adoption as if the placement of children in the homes of adopted parents was the beginning of their lives. When the children grow and come to understand biology and reproduction, they begin to realize that they did exist somewhere else *before* placement. Teens need to know what happened in the lives of their birth mothers that made an adoption placement necessary.

My question, "What do you want to know about your birth parents?" brought a definite, quick answer. I wasn't expecting this reply, and it continued to come as a surprise.

"I want to know why I was given up. that's all." Karen pressed her hands on the table and leaned toward me. "I just want to know why!" she said, emphasizing the question that so many teens had demanded of me. She was my twenty-second interview and it was the twenty-second time I'd heard, "I want to know why." It seemed to me that there were thousands of possible answers to "What do you want to know about your birth parents?" Teens could have said, "I want to know whether they had any more children," "I want to know whether they're healthy"—any number of things. But as I listened to Karen repeat for the twenty-second time, "Why was I given up for adoption?" I, the adoptive mother who had believed that love should be all that mattered, finally accepted that this question was of great importance.

Karen invited me into her large apartment in the suburbs of Vancouver. Her boyfriend and another friend were sitting on the living room rug listening to music; Karen and I walked into her kitchen and sat at the table to talk. Short and bright-eyed, Karen talked quickly, rushing through a conversation like an enthusiastic evangelist, as if there wasn't enough time to tell me everything. At twenty, she was the youngest of five children. The youngest three were adopted, but that didn't make it easier for her to accept her own adoption. When she learned at age twelve that she'd been adopted, Karen was very angry with her adoptive mother for not telling her when she was younger, and angry with her birth mother for abandoning her. She ran away, then returned. Her older sister had been sympathetic because she also had run away from home when she was younger. She told Karen that she had had the same feelings, but that adoption was something that didn't have to be negative. Although the sisters talked for a long time, Karen was still left with feelings of anger and "not being real."

When she ran away at fifteen, Karen hitchhiked across Canada, returned in a year, then ran away again. Finally her dad told her that she would have to leave home. Since she had been living on her own, she felt closer to her parents and brothers and sisters. She told me that she understood how difficult she had been for everyone, with her demands and questions, during those teen years.

Karen still had a tremendous need to find her birth mother. She wouldn't feel like a real person, she told me, until she knew who she was at the start of her life, and where she began. When that was resolved, she planned to go to school to become a zoologist. But, until she settled her beginnings, she didn't feel as though she could plan anything.

This need to "settle who I am," was strong for many of the teens I interviewed. It was as if they were riding a merry-go-round watching life drift past and unable to join it until they knew who they had been and where they belonged.

Responding sympathetically to Karen's need to know her past, I momentarily forgot that it was her reaction to this need that was paralyzing her. It wasn't the fact of her adoption that was stirring up her life, it was that she thought about adoption all the time. Because I truly liked and wanted to help her, I wanted to respond with positive assurance that she *ought* to know why she was given up for adoption, that in wanting to know her background she wasn't unreasonable or even unusual. Karen, who was such an interesting, stimulating person, overwhelmed me with her passion to be herself.

The need to know who their birth parents are doesn't seem to be related to how well teens get along with their adoptive parents or whether they rate them as good or inadequate as parents. Nor was this need related to age, sex, or position in the family. Only Ryan and Joanne did not think knowing why was of any great import.

Why a child was given up for adoption wasn't important to me until I started this project. Although grateful to the two birth mothers who had given sons to our family, I hadn't tried to put myself into their minds. I remembered what I had been told about why my sons had been placed for adoption and had a general idea of why they were given up. Wasn't that enough? As my sons grew up I learned that all I had been told about their background was not true, and that my sons needed to know the truth. The social worker's report was not enough for them.

What she had been told was not enough for Karen, either. "I think about it almost every day. When I get all the pieces together, I'll be satisfied. I look in the mirror and think, 'she probably looks like me.' I even asked someone once, a friend of my girlfriend's mother, if she was my mother. I knew she'd put a child up for adoption years ago and she sort of looked like me. She said she wasn't and I felt so stupid. I never did that again."

Karen, like many adopted teens, speculated on who her mother was. "I think my birth mother was Russian. She might have come over with a group of women that came from Russia to Alberta around that time. They all left again, so maybe she's back in Russia. I'll have to go through a lot to go over there and see her. If she's still living there it would be really hard to see her, but if she's still here, no problem."

I paused at that. Was she seriously considering travelling to Russia to find out who had given birth to her? She was. It seemed a drastic plan to me, but an adopted woman who read this manuscript commented, "I don't think that this is all that drastic. I'd have done it too." I still had a lot to learn.

Karen said, "Because I was born in Alberta all I have to do is write and they'll send me my mother's name. This doesn't mean I'll go find her. It just means I'm going to know her history and that'll help me to know things about me that I maybe need to know. I don't know if I'm the same as anybody else, but I really do feel lost. I sometimes feel that I don't know who I am. I don't know who I should be.

"Some friends say, 'Oh, come on. I know what it's like.' But no.

They don't know. They aren't adopted. Their parents didn't give them up. They didn't throw them out. It hurts, you know. I want to know why."

Karen had a great need to know who her birth mother was, but I wondered if it was her intense personality that made the question seem so vital. But over and over as I continued to listen to teens' stories, they told me that information about their birth mothers was often vital to their emotional well-being.

Leslie was quite a different personality from Karen, yet she had the same need. A queen-sized waterbed dominated the living area of her studio apartment; pictures and ornaments made it crowded yet comfortable. Rock music drifted from the radio on the kitchen counter. In spite of the relaxed, homey atmosphere she had created, Leslie did not appear relaxed, but more as if she were competently ready for a difficult interview. She was a determined, organized woman with a clipped way of speaking that made me feel as though I'd better be businesslike.

Leslie had discovered her adoption order at age twelve while rifling through her mother's private papers. Her adoptive mother was upset at her discovery; she felt that Leslie might leave her and return to her original parents if she knew she had been adopted. Leslie couldn't understand this; their fear that she wouldn't love them if she knew she was adopted didn't make sense. She had no desire to leave the people she loved to go to strangers, and she didn't understand why that wasn't obvious to her parents. Unlike Karen, Leslie didn't view her past with an emotional pull, but rather as a source of information.

That was my impression. But Leslie was very self-contained, and I couldn't know as a result of one meeting the depths of her emotions. She told me that she didn't feel rejected by her adoptive parents; she felt some rejection by her original parents, but had absolutely no desire to trade homes. Her adoptive parents might never have told her she was adopted if she hadn't found out for herself, they were so fearful of her reaction. Why can't everyone deal with life on the basis of facts? Leslie thinks her parents' attitude at the time was wrong, but it was their decision. "Mom and Dad thought they were right. They did what they thought was best."

Once Leslie knew she was adopted, she started asking questions and, when she was seventeen, began to look for her birth parents. She found her mother's name and got in touch with her sisters. Although she hasn't met her mother, she knows who and where she was. Her sisters told her that, of all the seven children, Leslie looks the most like her mother. That pleased Leslie.

"My mom had six children already and her husband wasn't my father, so she had to give me up because she didn't want him to know about me." Although Leslie knew most of her family background and had pieced together what she thought was the real story, she still wanted to know, straight from her birth mother, why she had been placed for adoption. "My sister didn't tell me much about it, but apparently my mother got pregnant from her boyfriend and her husband came back. My mother couldn't tell her husband she was pregnant, so she gave me up for adoption. Her husband was so mean if he'd found out he'd have killed her.

"It was a small town and I guess some people knew about it." If her mother had kept Leslie with her and left her husband, she would not have been able to support seven children. "And at that time they had to worry about neighbours. I still don't know who my father is. The only way I'd find out who my father is would be to go and meet my mother. . . . My sister told her that I'm all right. My sister was upset because she wasn't sure if I was going to upset my mother's life. Her husband would kill her even now. I know a lot about her and it doesn't really matter if I don't meet her. The only reason I would like to meet her is because I'd like to know who my father is . . . I still wonder why the people that had me before didn't want me." She was referring to her first adoptive placement. Leslie had been placed for adoption as an infant, given up again at six months of age, then placed for adoption with her present parents. "It gets really, really confusing. Especially if you don't have anyone to talk to."

Psychologists tell us that babies bond with their parents and that a disruption in the bonding process causes emotional withdrawal. Leslie had suffered two bonding interruptions—the first with her birth mother and the second with her original adoption placement. In spite of that, Leslie appeared to have a firm and deep attachment to her adoptive parents—proving the resilience of some children.

So much of the passion that the teens showed on the topic of adoption concerned the reasons why they had been placed for adoption.

They understood that sometimes birth mothers were too young and had no money to support a child; grandparents hadn't been willing to help support a baby; birth fathers couldn't or wouldn't help. Sometimes a mother kept her baby for a few months or a year until life got too complicated, difficult, or stressful. Birth mothers had been ignored by their families, ignored by government aid programs, cut off from work and support, from friends, from parties and fun, and often they were poor. Teens who were sixteen or seventeen themselves often found it understandable why a young mother would give up a baby.

When the teens I interviewed didn't know why they had been placed for adoption, they guessed:

"Maybe she was too young."

"Maybe she just didn't want a kid."

"Maybe it was a one-night stand and I was a boo-boo."

"I don't know. No one will tell me. I don't know why or even where I was for six months. No one knows why."

"I guess they were too young, didn't have any money, and couldn't handle it."

Some parents, and I'm ashamed to say I was one of them, avoid the issues by telling the child that they put in an order for her or him and some unidentified woman did the family a favour by carrying and delivering the child—a sort of baby catalogue ordering system. The implication is that their birth mother was never really the "mother." I hadn't realized how unrealistic that was or that by calling my children's mother "the lady who had you" I was taking away her character, individuality, and personality. When I met my youngest son's birth mother and heard from her how difficult it had been to give up her baby, and how she had loved him, I was humbled and ashamed. She did *not* have this child for me. What an incredibly arrogant attitude I'd had. She had him for his own sake, and I can only be grateful.

Teens told me that they wanted a personal connection with a real past, not with a vague, dehumanized idea. It was hard for them to get an accurate image of a real person in a real situation who actually existed with the limited information they receive, such as, "Five foot six inches, blue eyes, fifteen years old, and fair." Even those who had a clear idea and good records where the social worker explained why she thought they were placed for adoption wanted to hear it from their mother.

In some provinces and states, social workers may ask for a letter from the birth mother at the time of adoption explaining why she relinquished her child. Such a letter is supposed to be passed on to the adoptive parents. The information in the letter is then to be passed on to the child as he or she is growing up. Most teens I interviewed thought it would be great to have that kind of communication.

But there could be problems with this. The social worker may not receive a letter; if she does, she may not pass it on to the parents, or if the parents receive it, they may not pass the information on to the child. Wouldn't a name, address, and contact be better?

Almost any information would be welcome to some even if they didn't approve of the reason for placement. Many teens see their beginnings as rejection by their birth mother. There isn't any doubt that the act of giving up a baby for adoption can be seen as a great rejection, but that doesn't necessarily mean that the birth mother didn't want her baby. Giving up a baby and wanting that baby can exist together.

It is possible to want something desperately and know you cannot have it; to know it would not, in the long run, be wise. It's reasonable to think that giving up a child is hard. While I was a public health nurse, I met no one who was able to give up a child easily. Some cried for days. Some stoically left the hospital without tears, but that didn't mean their sorrow was any less deep. Part of the problem is that at childbirth your body and your heart are ready to nurture a child and you react badly to empty arms. It doesn't take a lot of imagination to empathize with how a birth mother would feel. It is not a clear case of rejection of the baby.

Mike saw adoption as rejection by his birth mother. He was fifteen years old, short, quiet, neatly dressed, and polite. He allowed me to interview him in the kitchen of his home as his sister bustled around getting ready for work, apologizing for being in the way. When the house was quiet and we had talked for a while, I asked Mike what he knew about his birth parents.

"Nothing. Mom and Dad don't know anything about them. I don't know anything."

"What do you want to know about your biological parents?"

"It would be kind of neat to know why they put me up for adoption." He paused. "And maybe, what ages they are. I don't think I want to meet them again. It'd be sort of scary. I might even know them already."

"What difference would knowing about your biological parents make?"

"It might take my mind off some of the things I've thought about." He looked at me seriously for a few moments and then leaned his head back against the wall. "Like, why did they put me up for adoption? Was I bad? Was it because of me?" I was startled, and then horrified, that he thought he was such a poor human being that his mother didn't want him.

"You think she thought you were bad?"

"Yeah. Sometimes I think that."

Mike didn't seem to be upset by this self-denigrating idea, but I was. "You know, Mike," I spoke very slowly, "it seems unlikely that a week-old baby did anything, *could* do anything to make its mother reject it."

Mike shrugged. "I don't know. Not really."

I tried again. "There is nothing you could have done that would make you bad. I mean a baby is just a baby. There's nothing you could have done that was wrong."

He nodded. I think it was a kind of thanks for my efforts, recognition that I had tried to understand. Mike was matter-of-fact about it, but I was upset that he could even *think* he was responsible for being given up.

Underneath this belief may be the fear that if he had been abandoned once because of who he was, he could be abandoned again. Wasn't there some way our society could prevent kids from having this kind of damaging speculation? Perhaps that letter from the birth mother explaining her reasons for surrendering him might help kids like him. Mike still feels that in some special way, he made his mother hate him so much that he wasn't worth keeping. Maybe he was so angry at her that it helped to imagine her as a cruel woman who would do something so rotten.

Understanding why a mother would give her child up for adoption became important to me. At this time I hadn't yet met my son's birth mother and I was struggling with issues around the desperation of birth mothers. I had talked to many mothers at the time of childbirth, but I wanted to know how a mother felt years later. I was privileged to get some interviews with birth mothers.

A dark, regal woman talked to me in her city home. She had

responded to my ad in the paper for teen interviews and thought I should hear what it was like from her point of view.

"We were engaged," she said of her partner, "but he gambled. I didn't think I could make enough money to support the baby and I didn't know whether what he and I had was going to last."

They eventually did marry and now have a family. It seemed busy and happy—two little girls and a dog kept running back and forth through the kitchen. When her first child was eighteen she searched for him, found him, and contacted his adoptive mother. The two mothers arranged for the son to meet his birth mother. He visits her occasionally now.

"It's nice that I know him. I always wondered and worried about him. In fact, I got depressed every year around his birth date. Now I know that he has a loving family who brought him up very well. And I know also that I will never really feel like his mother. I gave that position away. You can't do anything about the time you gave away. I'm glad I've met him, though. I feel better about the decision I made nineteen years ago and I think I've lost my depression." Their reunion reduced her guilt and allowed her to live with herself. Her son discovered where he fit in the pattern of his past.

When the discovery that you are adopted comes at the late age of twelve or thirteen, the rejection by the birth mother seems to be more difficult to handle. Karen learned of her adoption when she was twelve. Leslie also learned late and found it hard to understand. "I cried for a long time. Someone dumped me when I was a baby and I couldn't understand why."

Many teens told me that their resentment is not directed primarily at their birth mother, but at their adoptive mother (not their father) for not being honest with them. They trusted their (adoptive) mother to care for them, and when she withheld important information, they felt betrayed. She was supposed to love them and treat them fairly, and she lied.

Most teens felt that their birth information was their right. They felt adoptive parents were not fair or honest when they kept information to themselves. And, as Leslie said, "So what's the big deal? It's my background, isn't it?" Government officials and adoptive parents are slowly beginning to agree with Leslie's statement, but many still try to deny that teens existed anywhere before they joined their adopted family.

Some teens who knew quite a lot about their biological parents were happy to tell me about it. They saw themselves as coming from one place, the place of the birth mother, and moving to another, the adoptive home. Those who didn't know saw the time before their birth as a mystery. Am I the child of a celebrity who was forced by her career to abandon me? Is the woman who works in Sears downtown who looks like me, my mother? Is that woman coming down the street? Was I born at all or did I just arrive? They don't seriously believe that they came from outer space, but the joking comments indicate that they are uncomfortable, a little afraid that somehow they are not "normal." They wonder, worry, and imagine the best beginnings they could have—and the worst.

Leslie insisted that I understand. "Like you walk down the street and you see someone with brown eyes and brown hair, and you wonder, 'Gee, I wonder if they could be related to me?' You could walk right up to your mother. There was one time . . . a girl in a drugstore walked up to me and said, 'You know what? If you had your hair cut the same way as my sister you could be identical twins.' And *that* made me think—I wonder if I've got brothers and sisters. They could be right here under my nose and I'd never know it. 'Wanting to know' is just a kind of a feeling. Like there's a piece of the puzzle missing. Whether it's good or bad, you feel you have to know. You're compelled to know.

"That [knowledge of her birth parents] is part of me. that's part of my life. Whether I was too young to remember or not. . . . I was born in that hospital from one woman and I was given to another. . . . " Her voice drifted into silence. Then she said, "And I just want to know why."

I thought about why we, society, haven't kept the information these teens need. There were reasons—attitudes, and the real and imagined desires of both the birth parents and adopted parents. I remember the lawyer asking me if I wanted to know the name of my oldest son's birth mother. Because I was young, insecure, self-protecting, it didn't occur to me at the time that my son might eventually want to know and, by then, the information had been lost. All of society concerned with adoption except the adopted baby, helped shape our attitudes and approach to adoption. Our understanding of the needs of adopted children and teens has been imperfect.

Chapter 2

The Significance of Adoption

Teens

MOST TEENS I INTERVIEWED saw adoption as a good way to give homes to children who needed them. It was too bad that they had had to leave their birth parents, but they were glad they had ended up in their adoptive home. It seemed a right and reasonable process, but they knew that not everyone felt this way.

During the junior-high years many were teased— "Your mother didn't love you," and "You're weird"—because they were adopted. While this teasing hurt at the time, it wasn't widespread and stopped as they and their friends grew older. No one reported problems over adoption with friends or neighbours at the time of the interview. They told me that adoption made no difference to their chances in life or to the way they were treated outside of their homes.

The teens seemed indifferent to questions about social prejudice and, since I had assumed they met quite a lot of prejudice, it took repeated answers of, "No one treats me any different because I'm adopted," and "It doesn't make any difference," before I believed them. In the great democratic surge of the teen years where trying to fit in is so important, they would rather ignore differences than talk about them. Perhaps prejudice is something that becomes more obvious and yet more subtle as we get older. As well, prejudice against adoption is not socially correct. While theoretically adoption is a socially-approved cultural process, there seems to exist a strong bias toward "natural families," "blood ties," and "ancestral memories." Our acceptance of an adopted person's need to find his or her biological family is based on the assumption that biological families belong together.

This bias toward biological families operates in direct contradiction to our apparent acceptance of adoption. No wonder teens don't want to talk about it. The contradiction is confusing and unsettling. In order to feel secure, teens must rely on society's acceptance of adoption as a normal cultural practice, while at the same time knowing that biological families are preferred.

The teens I interviewed had very few problems with brothers and sisters about their adoption, but two told me that they had a grandmother who couldn't accept them as part of the family. In both cases, their parents explained that the grandmother was old and wrong. "Grandma's a little crazy; you're all right." As in many cases where rejection is part of life, it was easier to deal with it when acceptance and support came from those closest to them.

The teens had friends, cousins, and neighbours who were adopted. There are more children adopted today than thirty years ago. None of my sixty-five first cousins were adopted. My children have fourteen cousins, five of whom were adopted. I took an invisible flight down the street where I lived at the time and did a census. Two of my children were adopted; my first neighbour had three children she bore herself; the next neighbour had one biological child and one adopted child; the next had one adopted child, then a biological one; the woman at the corner had two biological children who were stepchildren to her husband. Families today tend to be combinations of biological, adopted, step- and foster-children more often than they were even ten years ago. When teens are younger, as Kerri said, they sometimes feel as if they are the only adopted child in the world, but by the time they are fifteen or sixteen they know others.

The teens saw adoption as a positive process—every one of them told me that they would adopt children themselves. Some didn't see themselves in a position to do so for many years; some said they wanted to have biological children first—but all said they would adopt. Many felt that they would be better parents to an adopted child than their own had been.

"I would understand," Rhea said emphatically. "I'm going to adopt. And I'm going to foster children, too. Because there are just too many children in this world who don't have a decent home or some place to say, 'This is where I can come and touch down when things get too rough.' Anyway, I figure I know how to do it. Oh, yes. You bet! I'll adopt." This enthusiasm for being an adoptive parent stems from their own experiences, and indicates that these teens think adoption is a socially acceptable and responsible option for families.

While her ideas were similar to Rhea's, nineteen-year-old Sarah came to her conclusions through a good home and loving attention from her adoptive parents. "My parents did a good job [on me], so I can too. For sure I'm going to adopt."

Sarah arranged to see me at her parents' apartment in a busy section of Vancouver close to downtown. She was blonde, fair-skinned, and the only child of loving parents. Married recently, she now lived with her husband three hundred miles north and was visiting her parents for a short holiday in the city.

Sarah knew quite a lot about her birth parents. Her adoptive parents had read the social worker's history and remembered much of what they had read. When Sarah was fourteen, her adoptive mother told her everything she knew. Sarah knew what kind of a person her birth mother was, where she worked, that she had a sixteen-year-old daughter, what her father was like, and what work he did—though not his name. She knew that her sixteen-year-old sister had offered to quit school and look after her, that her mother just couldn't support two children, that she had no one to help her.

Sarah's adoptive mother did what many fail to do. She progressed from the "chosen child" story of the younger years—the simple explanation given to inquiring four- to six-year-olds—and developed the explanation of Sarah's adoption into the more complex and detailed history that teens' need.

Although she knew her birth mother's name, address, and telephone number, Sarah didn't plan to contact her. And while she was happy with her start in life and knew her adoptive parents loved her, she realized that all adoptees didn't feel the same. She felt every one had a right to know who he or she was and to be comfortable with that knowledge. Her own comfort level may have been a combination of an easy-going temperament and her parents' attention to the importance of adoption and adoption information in Sarah's life. She wanted to meet her birth mother if that was agreeable to her, but she would not barge into her life without some indication of welcome.

Sarah could have called on one of several adoption services in her area. But such services for adoptees are not a routine part of life that are available with the aura of entitlement that comes with eye examinations or routine dental check-ups. No one arranges every year or two for the adoptee to have the opportunity to talk about issues of their development. If they did, all members of the adoption triangle—children, adoptive parents, and birth parents—would probably have much greater understanding of the effects of adoption.

Sarah has strong feelings for her adoptive parents, believing that the parent-child relationship is an emotional one that develops, rather than a biological one that just exists. She had resolved many of the questions about adoption in a timely way as she grew through her teen years and was comfortable, as many teens are, with her adoptive status. Her parents had given her a good childhood and she looked forward to the future.

It is easy to understand that emotions may be hidden, but physical appearance would, one would think, be obvious. Not so. Adopted children often do not notice that they look different from their adoptive family until approaching the teen years. Differences in physical appearance are accepted by younger children easily; it is adults and teens who apply character traits to physical appearance. Information about birth families gives adopted children a sense of physical connection to others who look similar. Those teens who had information about their biological parents said such things as, "My mother was tall and had hair like mine," with a kind of pride. They also gave their ethnic origin, "I'm Russian, actually," as if it was a label that established their identity. We all spend at least some time as a teenager trying to figure out who we are, how we feel about life, what values and actions are right for us. A sense of belonging in this family, in this school, in this community, and even to this human race is established (or not) more during the teen years than at any other developmental stage. It's normal to want to know how you fit into life.

Those teens who are obviously a different race from their parents or from their brothers and sisters find that this need for an identity gains significance as they grow older. They may be in their late teens before they realize there is a difference, or they may have noticed it at a very early age. There isn't a magic age at which they suddenly notice that their skin is brown and their adoptive mother is white. Some children always know, but it isn't significant to them until they gain awareness of the role of race in society and come up against society's prejudice. If their family believes that they are wonderful as they are, they will have less problem with prejudice than if their family believes that they are somehow inferior because of their race.

Many families today try to give their children some knowledge and understanding of their ethnicity, race, and birth culture. While it isn't realistic or even possible for them to offer the same environment and cultural richness of the birth family, adoptive parents can provide enough information so that children will feel comfortable with people of their own race as they grow up and leave home.

In North America and Europe, adopted teens are most often non-white—Black or Native American or Korean—in a family that is white. Once, I met an aboriginal woman who had a white daughter; I was a white woman with an aboriginal son. We laughed about our family portraits—negatives or positives of each other. But most often, if the teen's race differs from her adoptive parents, she is usually a minority race. In some areas of the country, this is easily accepted; in other areas such a teen will meet prejudice and racial discrimination. It helps to remember, as one teen said to me, that "prejudice is the other person's problem," although prejudice can become a very difficult problem for teens.

There are organizations that promote cultural and racial identity. Teens who are of a different ethnicity or race from their adoptive parents may want to join one so that they can meet people who look like themselves, and can learn from them.

How much background information should an adopted child receive? Some argue that adopted children should not know their beginnings because some stories may be unhappy. The teens I interviewed did not agree. If they didn't know their information, they could easily imagine it as very bad. Most adopted teens have friends who are in difficult circumstances: living with a divorced mother because their father is an alcoholic or moved in with another woman; or living with a father because their mother has left the family. Dealing with trouble, learning to live in a loving relationship even when rejected by one parent, and learning to like yourself, are part of teen life. Teens told me that they could handle their slice of life as well as anyone else.

As Leslie said, "Everyone else has that kind of information. Why can't I have it? What is it, some kind of big secret? Or is it so bad that someone, somewhere is keeping it from me?"

Most teens I interviewed were not concerned that they had very little information on their medical backgrounds. All had been told that their parents were in good health. It seems unlikely that *all* the parents of so many adopted teens were without *any* medical problems and more likely that the reporting of the medical history wasn't accurate. One was born premature, one had had pneumonia, but the rest seemed to have had a disease-free background . . . with one exception. One teenager knew that a grandparent had died of cancer. That meant 199 grandparents were disease-free.

At the time they were born, most of their birth parents were under twenty-five. Many of *their* parents were under fifty and no medical history was obtained further than that generation. Heart disease, cancer, adult diabetes, cataracts, and various other hereditary ailments most often develop after fifty years of age. The teens generally accepted their disease-free history. Only Leslie and Nicole wondered if their history had been accurate. One young woman who had been trying to have a child wanted to know her birth mother's child-bearing history because her doctor kept asking for information she didn't have.

Some teens worried that they might inherit mental illness. While some mental diseases such as a tendency to schizophrenia and depression may be inherited, and since adopted children often don't know their medical history, they worry that this is part of their background. There are studies that show a higher incidence of psychopathology in *adoptive parents* than parents who have not adopted (Holden, 1991). The researcher voiced surprise that adoptive parents who had been assessed for their suitability as parents, demonstrated psychopathology. So it may not be heredity that predisposes adopted children to mental illness, but the environment they live in—their adoptive families.

Suicide rates are higher in adolescent adoptees than non-adoptees (Boult, 1988; Robinson 1991), but studies indicate that while the tendency to impulsive behaviour may be inherited, the actual suicide is a choice that is linked to social and environmental factors, and may be more because of social attitudes to adoption than to heredity. Again, this phenomenon may be linked to the relations between the child and his or her adoptive parents.

Eating disorders are more prevalent in adopted children than non-adopted. This may reflect the lack of belief in their identity and low self-esteem rather than an inherited predisposition.

While teens need information about their birth families so that they can establish their identity, they also need it to better understand their own capabilities and limitations. If a teen's biological family has many members who are alcoholics, the teen will be better able to deal with an addictive body that cannot tolerate the kind of "weekend drinking" that many of their friends can. Information about tendencies and predispositions in their biological families could help teens make better-informed choices.

B.E. Boult (1988) describes some of the fears in adopted adolescents, which include those about the moral character of their birth mother and her rejection of them, that their adopted status might be temporary if their adoptive parent decided to give them away, and feeling alienated but unable to talk to parents about it. Their fears are all ones that adoptive parents can address, so they are not inevitable, not genetically programmed into the child. These problems have been caused by a society obsessed with secrecy and taboos in the adoption process, particularly the lack of open discussion about adoption. In my work with suicidal teens, I found that fulfilling the need to belong in their family and the ability to talk to someone, preferrably their parents, was strongly preventative of suicide. Adoptive parents who are more likely to be psychically pathological, a society that causes confusion by withholding information about where the adopted child belongs, along with the underlying problem of not being able to talk to parents, combine to result in a greater incidence of suicide. If parents understand the real need of teens to talk and the way in which that talking and parents' listening can help prevent suicide, the higher rate of suicide among adopted teens may decrease.

Were teen boys any different from teen girls in how they felt about being adopted? Boys who had been adopted seemed to have the same rate of criminal behaviour as the general population, but higher than the population of adoptive parents (Howe, 1998). Girls seemed to have rates more nearly co-related to their adoptive parents. Generally, boys have more learning problems than girls. Studies show that adopted children achieve as well and even better than non-adopted children (Maughan & Pickles, 1990), yet we are still concerned about the likelihood of learning disabilities, anxiety, and hostile behaviour patterns (Howe, 1998) in adopted boys. Studies show that adoptees are as successful when they are adults as non-adoptees, but the teen years are often more difficult.

How teenaged boys felt was about being adopted was important to me. Were there differences between boys and girls other than those the researchers pointed out? I had the impression, so far, that boys just didn't concern themselves with adoption very much. Was this because my sons refused to discuss it, or because boys are generally taught by our society not to discuss emotions? Was it true that boys really didn't care as much?

Fifteen-year-old John lived at home with his adoptive parents, two sisters, and one brother. No one else in the family was adopted. He was tall, lanky, quiet, a good student in high school, and planned to get a law degree. While interested in adoption—he answered my ad in the paper—he didn't seem worried about it. The information he had on his background told him that during the first fourteen months of his life, he had been placed in several different foster homes. Neither he nor his (adoptive) mother knew why. The curiosity most often felt about birth parents was shared by John. He wanted to meet them, see what kind of people they were, and find out if he had any brothers and sisters.

John said he would eventually marry and have children. He would adopt children, he told me; he could tell his son what it was like. "I could tell him I went through the same things"—the wondering, the talks with his parents. He'd understand his own son's need to do all that. John appeared calm and level-headed and while he had had concerns in the past and talked them out with his parents, he didn't tell me what those concerns were. Perhaps John's greatest stability comes from the his ability to talk easily with his parents.

Mike had been worried that he hadn't been wanted in the first place. Alex had worried that there might be hereditary mental illness in his biological family. The twins told me there was no problem with adoption. Bill desperately wanted to find some biological family connections after being rejected by his adopted parents. The young men I interviewed had many different concerns. I couldn't assume my sons' reluctance to talk about adoption was in any way typical. In fact, I couldn't assume from the teens I interviewed that the boys were any different from the girls in their attitudes and concerns.

Maryann, sixteen, worked split-shift at a fast food restaurant and had three free hours before going back to her job. She threw a jacket over her uniform and climbed into my van in the parking lot where we sat out of the rain. She was slight, short, and spoke in teen dialect, the jerky shorthand that made her story seem all the more spontaneous. Slow to start, once she began telling me how she felt, she talked for a long time without urging. She had lived through difficult years between the ages of thirteen and sixteen, leaving home several times, feeling desperate, overdosing on drugs, and generally trying many ways of getting away from her family. She felt anchorless, drifting without direction, floundering around Children's Aid, social workers, and her parents. At this time, she was trying to get Children's Aid to support her in an independent apartment. Maryann wanted to be in charge of her life; she thought she did better when she was living away from authority.

When she is eighteen, Maryann wants to find her birth mother, but not her birth father. Her adoptive parents were willing to help, although her father was worried that rejection by her birth mother would hurt Maryann. Her adoptive mother didn't think that would happen, but rather that, since her birth mother kept Maryann for six months before placing her for adoption, she cared and would probably be willing to talk to her.

Knowing her birth family was very important to Maryann. She thought her aimlessness had something to do with the fact that she didn't really feel entitled to her place in society.

Although Maryann still wants to know her birth mother and her name, she thought of her adoptive parents as her parents, even though she didn't want to live with them. She said that if she could make it through high school and get into a university, she planned first to be a medical doctor, then a psychiatrist who works with delinquent kids. She understood what it felt like to be alienated. "A lot of kids feel that adopted kids are not really people; that's their attitude. They want to know how you deal with being given up. They're curious, I guess. My family treats me okay now. I get some negative feeling from my grandma because I'm adopted. When I was younger that hurt, but my mom put her down for it. One uncle and aunt are okay. My friends and neighbours don't care about adoption. They treat me okay. No problem there." She was clear about who did and who did not accept her.

"When I was thirteen I tried to commit suicide. I took a bunch of pills. I really hated my [adoptive] mother to the point that I wanted to get out and get away. You know what I mean? I had a teacher who took me to the hospital. After that I had social workers and psychiatrists and I was knocked around from social worker to social worker and I was starting to hate them, you know what I mean?

"I've got one at Poplars now that I had from grade nine at St. John's. I mean we just don't get along at all. I sit down and it's the same questions she asks every week. I don't know. It's stupid, sometimes. You see it was strange, because I didn't know I was overdosing. Like I was just blank. I was taking them [pills] all day; I took them in class. I mean I had them because I was up to ten or fifteen aspirins a day—every day. Plus stress pills. It was kind of like a high all day. It made me relax. Then, after a while, I was just taking them and taking them. I had a bottle on my desk and I took all the pills in the bottle."

Maryann sat in silence for a moment and watched the summer rain stream down the windshield of my van. "The thing is, now I've got a problem. I'm living out of the house [at her sister's] and I've got to find another place to live. So now I have to go down to Children's Aid again and get mixed up with all their stupid social workers and everything. It's going to be a real pain. I mean, when I was younger I went to Children's Aid to get out of the house. And what they wanted to do was have a family get-together, you know? My dad and my sister were willing to go, but my mom wasn't. She said it was my problem, not hers. She didn't want nothing to do with it, eh? So I don't know. It's a money problem now. I can't live off my dad. I don't know what's happening now."

Maryann couldn't talk her problems out with her mother, possibly because she didn't know how, or because her mother wouldn't listen.

While many teens have difficult relationships during these years, adopted teens have the added problem of always being unsure of their status as a family member. This can result in the "striving for perfection" behaviour of some teens and the testing "will you love me if I'm bad" behaviour of others. Some adopted teens believe that they are "bad" and that as soon as their parents discover this, or as soon as they are bad enough, they will be rejected again. This feeling of alienation, of disentitlement within the family, causes emotional insecurity, anxiety, and a lack of trust in the parents' ability to support and sustain them. Some parents believe that their adopted children require constant reassurance that they are loved, and that, no matter what the parents do and say, it is never enough.

I'm not sure at what point my oldest son began to believe in my support and love, but I remember after a particularly difficult time when he was eighteen, screaming at him, "Loving you is a life sentence!" In spite of my anger and frustration, I believe he realized that I was his mother forever, whether he was "good" or "bad."

Maryann was still going through the difficult years. "When I go in there [to Children's Aid]," she said, "I don't know what they're going to say. 'Cause if I go in there, they're not going to shove me in no home." Maryann was adamant, "that's for sure. I mean if I go in there and they say, 'Well, we'll stick you in this home,' I don't know, I'd rather live on the streets. It's not as if I'm up to anything most of the time, you know. I mean most of my life now is just working, going home [to her sister's place], sleeping, working, going home, sleeping. So I mean it's not as if I'm up to anything. I'm happier now. For some reason inside of me, I feel a lot better now I'm out of the house."

We watched the rain, cocooned in my van, thinking about the problems of being sixteen and adopted. My son David poked his head out of the Dairy Queen. I waved. He ducked back inside.

"Sometimes being adopted doesn't affect my life at all and sometimes it does. You know, sometimes I think, 'When I find her [birth mother], I'm really going to wring her neck. She ain't going to hear the end of me.'" She smiled and shrugged. "Adoption isn't going to affect me. It won't bother me at all."

While Maryann told me this I thought of her feelings of alienation, or not being real, of not belonging. At some point soon, I hoped, she would understand that her feelings may be related to her being adopted.

"My mom and dad treat me like they would if they'd had me. I mean, I *can* go back home. I mean, even though she kicked me out, now she doesn't mind if I go back home. But now that I know what it's like being out, I don't want to go back. I've been out of the house two months now—after the end of grade ten. I lived with a friend for two weeks and they were going to keep me, but me and my friend started not to get along, you know how that happens, so I moved in with my sister and now my sister and I aren't getting along. She keeps saying, 'When are you going to move out? When are you going to move out?'

I live with her and her boyfriend. My mom doesn't think I'm going to get anywhere. I'm a number one skipper-outer. I don't know. . . ."

It is hard for teens to have faith in themselves when their mother does not believe in them, or when they think she doesn't. As well, Maryann was dealing with the age-old problem of trying to define herself as separate from her parents, as a person in her own right. This common teen task may be complicated by the perception of most adopted teens that she had *never* been allowed to be herself, to define herself truly, but had always had to assume a position as a child of the adoptive family. She may have been be able to accept that position intellectually, but emotionally she didn't feel authentic.

I asked Maryann if she would adopt children herself." Yes, because I think I'd understand what an adopted child is going through at certain times and ages. Compared to what parents do that weren't adopted. Like my sister [a biological child] wants to adopt. But you know I just hope she'll understand."

David was patiently waiting under the eaves of the Dairy Queen, hands in his pockets, hunched over as he tried to keep the rain away. Feeling guilty for being warm and dry, I opened the door, called, and he dashed through the rain to the van, nodded to Maryann as she left, and settled in for the drive. I forgot to turn the tape off and have a record of David criticizing my driving with the acumen and theoretical expertise of a twelve-year-old all the way back to my friend's house.

Suzanne, mentioned previously, at fourteen years had had great difficulty in believing that she belonged in her family. Her mother had told me that Suzanne was "difficult . . . a handful." Slim, blonde, and beautiful, Suzanne was also intelligent and sad. She found it hard to talk to me, difficult to tell me what she was thinking. Speaking hesitantly, softly, she took time between sentences to decide whether to reveal anything to me at all. The youngest of three children, Suzanne was the only adopted child and the only girl. In spite of what ought to have been a privileged position, she felt as if she was treated as an outsider in her own family. She didn't get along with either her mother or her father and thought that she would never be good enough to fit in. In some ways she felt lucky to have a family that could give her food, clothing, and an education, but, in other ways, she felt the isolation wasn't worth it. At twelve, she had run away from and stayed away for a year. When she returned, nothing had changed. She still felt unwanted, unaccepted, not quite what the family had expected. What she didn't tell me at the time of the interview was that her adoptive father was sexually abusing her.

Suzanne often had a different opinion from the rest of the teenagers I interviewed. "Yes, I'd adopt. I'd treat my children as I wanted to be treated as a kid. I'd let them know everything about their parents." And then, on second thought, said, "But then maybe I wouldn't adopt, because I don't want my children to carry the worry of wondering about their natural parents. I don't want that to be between us."

Adoption seems to be a reasonable possibility to most teens. This doesn't mean that they aren't independent thinkers—they have come to their understanding of adoption by puzzling it out for themselves. Adoption was not a subject that was often discussed in the classroom or the school yard except as a curiosity. This was one reason why so many were anxious to talk to me; they seldom had anyone else to talk to about it. Even when they felt secure in their social situation, and even though they felt adoption was a reasonable, realistic social process, they didn't talk about it. Some felt that talking about adoption was somehow "disloyal" or "hurtful" to their adoptive parents. I had thought that my sons didn't talk to me much about adoption because they didn't care about it. But the teens I interviewed made me realize that I couldn't presume that. They told me my sons probably *wouldn't* talk to me about it.

The teenage years are tough times with parents. Many told me that their parents were uninformed, too critical, too demanding. But when asked to rate their (adoptive) parents out of ten (ten being high and one, low), seventy-five percent rated their parents between eight and ten while twenty-five percent rated them six or less. Even those who had stormy years with parents, who had run away from home or had been unhappy, didn't always rate parents low. "They really tried," one girl told me. "I was an awful kid. I'm really glad now that I came back and tried again because they really cared."

Karen said of her family, "I get along great with them now. In the past year, now I do. Like, now I love them more than ever. When I was fifteen and up to now, I didn't care what they said about my life because they were wrong. Because as far as I was concerned they didn't know me. I felt a natural mother had a certain touch with her own child-like she kind of knew things about her own child." She had absorbed the social bias that biological families are best, that adoptive families are a substitute.

"That's what I thought then," Karen continued. "So I figured they [adoptive parents] didn't know anything about me and talking to them was a waste of time. And it *was* a waste of time to me. There's only two people—you and my sister—that I have actually wanted to talk to—wanted to tell these things about adoption."

For some adopted children, the fear of abandonment is so strong that they push away those who are closest to them, often their adoptive mother. While this fear may not be conscious, it influences their lives and may motivate their behaviour. If they do something awful enough, their mother might reject them. They believe at some level that since they have been rejected before, their adoptive mother will reject them, too. Rather than waiting for that to happen, they try to provoke it."

"Me and my parents," Karen said, "we haven't sat down yet—to this day, actually—to see how I feel. It was such a huff when I wanted to find my real mother. No one had the . . . calmness to actually get into deep discussion with me. So like, my [adoptive] mother told me that because of the fact that I was the last child, and she'd been through so many things with the other four: sex, managing money, and things like that, just the ways of life period . . . she didn't talk about those things with me.

"I'm just starting to get myself on my feet. But still I'm not stable enough. I'm too emotional. Anything just hits me and I blow up like a fire hydrant."

I gave her credit for at least being able to feel.

"I know how to feel, all right. I'm getting pretty sick of all this feeling. I'm having trouble accepting love, too. I know there's something inside me I have to deal with. Because my own [birth] mother couldn't keep me, I thought she didn't love me. I still think she didn't love me. This is why, when somebody tells me they love me or somebody tries to show me they love me, I reject it."

When the teens told me that they would have families of their own, would adopt children or have biological children, they usually left out this piece of emotional development that Karen was talking about—the idea that they could trust a loving relationship. The sense of trust develops in the first years of life. If the adopted child had bonds of love that were broken or disrupted in those years, he or she may need to work hard at dealing with this before creating a new family of their own.

Karen's boyfriend who had been listening to records in the living room was an immediate problem. She wasn't just projecting that she'd have problems with trust in the future—her boyfriend was here, and her problem was now. "You know, I need so much proof—unreasonable proof—because of the fact. . . . It all bears down to my mother. That is the problem."

Many adoptees, most of whom are less articulate than Karen, have the same problem. Having once been abandoned, with the disruption of bonding that that entails, they fear being abandoned again. Like Karen, they know that loss is part of life, that people may love them and leave them, and that they are probably lovable. But they *feel* unlovable, that there is something inherently wrong with them that will cause abandonment in the future. Every relationship becomes tainted with this fear. Not all adoptees have this strong a fear, and some don't seem to have it at all. But some, like Karen, who is not pathological—sick or emotionally ill—have an early-set fear of being abandoned. This fear exists together with a relief at having been placed in their adoptive home. It is not a comfortable juxtaposition and one that adoptees must tease out, talk about, and attempt to resolve.

Karen was gaining awareness of herself. Adoptive parents, social workers, and society in general have not been very understanding about the grieving that adoptees need to do for their lost mothers, and the resolution they must have over their first separation. Most people believe that if the separation was at a young age, surely babies don't feel the loss. Apparently they do.

"I don't have a lot of self-confidence. I'm twenty and I don't even have my grade twelve. If you don't have grade twelve you don't have much self-confidence. I need a lot of people saying to me, 'Oh, you look good.' I need to build my life so I have something to make me feel good. This is why I'm doing this [getting her grade twelve diploma], so I have something to feel good about myself. Now I feel I do everything wrong."

When I asked Karen if she felt she was part of her family or if anyone in her family treated her differently because she was adopted, she said, "I thought my relatives treated me differently, but you know it was probably just me. I mean I even do that to this day. I see things that aren't really happening. It's just my perspective. I always thought that the natural ones were getting treated the best and we were getting the worst of it all. My family is very strong, very career-oriented, all of them. They're all affectionate, all loving. My family is super. There's nothing wrong with them—now. When I was giving trouble against my mother, my family was giving it right back. And it wasn't good then. I was a rotten child. I was rotten. I pulled a knife on my brother, like for hitting my sister. Things like that."

I had a sudden surge of sympathy for Karen's parents. I looked straight at her. Her eyes twinkled in understanding and she nodded. "I really was a rotten kid. When we were younger we were all so close in age, my mother said this is why we went through all this. The only way I figured I was ever going to get out of my situation was to scrap my way out of it.

"I always figured I was a rebel. I met a lot of people who scrapped with me and I wasn't going to be 'Miss Sweetness' and sit back and smile. I was going to scrap right back.

"I think when I ran away from home [at fifteen] and hitch-hiked across Canada, I learned a lot—some things good, some things not so good—but I was independent. At that time I was doing what I wanted to do and no one was going to tell me any different and no one was ever going to tell me I was wrong because I never gave anybody a chance. Even now, when someone tells me I'm doing something wrong, I rebel against it. I say, 'Forget it. I can do what I want. I can say what I please.' My family knows that now. My mom knows that. She will not argue with me now."

The trouble Karen and her family went through resulted in more secure emotional support for her. "I finally realized that they [her adoptive parents] brought me up. My family is super now. My sister talked to me; she said that she went through the same resentment. The feeling of being alone. I mean, like, 'Who are you? Your own mother gave you up. What was the matter with you?' She told me that she put my mother and family through hell, too. She finally realized that they brought her up; they clothed her and fed her and comforted her. The alternative was foster care. At one time she wanted to find her parents, but she doesn't even want to meet her birth mother now. Mom is Mom, born through her or not, because that's who she was raised with. I couldn't understand that then. But I understand it now."

Karen and her sister had come to an intellectual understanding of their entitlement to their positions in the family and, perhaps, an emotional acceptance as well. They were caught in the anger and resentment between their first separation and gratitude for their adoptive home. To be accepted by their adoptive family, they had to be relinquished by their birth mothers, which caused uncomfortable and contradictory feelings. If all the members of the adoption triangle—birth mother, adoptive parents, and adoptee—had understood the need for reassurance and the need to feel secure in the family, Karen may not have had such stormy teen years.

When I asked teens to evaluate their parents, they were realistic. If they rated their parents below five on the one-to-ten scale, it was usually for a serious reason such as abuse, or a cold attitude, or a lack of caring. No one who had only the usual problems of interfering mothers or demanding fathers rated parents below five, except Katy, who told me she was having a particularly rough time with her (adoptive) mother.

Everyone felt that their parents owed the same kind of responsibilities to their adopted children as to biological children. There should be no differences between them. Only Suzanne felt that there *was* a difference between herself and her brothers who were biological children. She thought there *shouldn't* be any difference, but that there was. No one else saw any differences and no one expected that there would be any differences. Some thought their parents should be more understanding and help them to find their beginnings, their birth parents, or information about their birth parents.

"If they accept me as their child, then they accept the fact that I am adopted and that I have a different history from them. If they accept me, they can't ignore the fact that I'm adopted." Rhea was emphatic about that.

When I asked what teens thought the responsibilities of a child to his adoptive parents were, all of them told me that the child had the same responsibilities as a biological child: the child owes a duty to the parents; the parents owe a duty to the child.

What about the second set of parents in the adoption triangle? Teens started life with another set of parents. What are these parents' responsibilities to them?

"They should let me know who they are. Nothing more." Dora said after pondering the question.

Rhea thought differently. "I think they owe me my background and the reason why they gave me up. At least that. But not their names, or where they live now."

Lena believed that the responsibilities of her biological parents were over. "I'm here and that's pretty well all they needed to do for me, give me to a good home."

Leslie said, "My mother owes me something. She should tell me who my father is. If she doesn't want to tell me, that's her prerogative. I'm not going to fight her for it. But she ought to tell me." Leslie knew her birth mother's name, where she lived, and quite a lot about her.

Katy wanted to know why she was given up. She felt her birth parents owed her a reason. "Not an explanation exactly, or an excuse or anything really involved—just why. I also want to know if there are any loonies in the family."

Most of the teens did not feel that their birth parents owed them anything at all. Nor did they feel they owed anything to their birth parents.

"No, definitely not. No. I don't owe them anything," was the usual reply. Only fourteen-year-old Katy felt an obligation to her birth parents. "I owe it to them to grow up to be responsible; to lead my life right. Not to screw up. They put me up for adoption because they didn't think they could bring me up in an environment that would be positive. They put me in a good home and they probably want to see me grow up to be a responsible person."

Rhea felt that she had a responsibility not to disrupt her birth mother's life. "I should give her a guarantee that I'm not going to cause problems or seek revenge for her giving me up."

Dora said the same thing in a different way. "I feel an obligation to let them live their own lives." No one else felt any obligation to their birth parents.

These opinions were offered before the teens had met or knew their birth parents except for Rhea, who had ongoing contact with her birth mother. There may be a time when as adults, the teens will have different perspectives about any obligation to birth parents.

In my youngest son's life, his birth mother gives him his place in the feast halls of his aboriginal community. His place depends on her. He is then part of a culture and tradition that has obligations and responsibilities which may involve him. Adoption is a common practice in his culture. Other adoptees may find themselves part of a large family, or the only child of a single parent, and responsibilities may become more real and more obvious. Because teens saw no obligation to birth parents at this time in their lives does not mean that they will never feel any obligation.

I asked teens what difference it would make to their lives if they knew their birth parents.

Katy said, "I want to know them. More than anything, I want to know who they were; what they were like—their lifestyle; if they are alive. That bothers me, seeing as you have to wait until you're nineteen to find them. that's a long time. It wouldn't make much difference, really, knowing about them. I wouldn't put my parents down—like I wouldn't forget about them and go and live with my natural parents. They [her adoptive parents] are the parents that brought me up and they're the ones I'd stay with," Katy said, although at this time, she thought her adoptive mother was old-fashioned, too strict, and didn't understand her at all. "My natural parents didn't have to put up with me as a baby. They didn't have to bring me up. It's the truth."

Paul didn't know if it would make much difference. "I'd like to watch them for a week—be invisible or something so I could see what their life is like without them seeing me. I wouldn't intrude unless . . . I don't think I would intrude. I'd like to know who they are and what they're doing."

Nicole wanted to know "What they look like and that's it. I would be concerned about invading their privacy now. I don't think it's important [to meet them] because I know basically the reason I was put up for adoption and I'm quite willing to accept that. But I want to know what they look like, to see why I look the way I do, stuff like that. I was given a description of height, hair colour, eye colour on the forms, but I'd like to see for myself."

Eighteen-year-old Sherry wanted to know about her birth mother. "I'd just like to meet her some day. I'd like to know what she looks like. She might not want to see me, but if I could just meet her and talk to her, I'd like that."

John, fifteen, was systematic about his needs. "I'd like to meet them. See what kind of people they are. I'd like to know their occupations, where they live, and what they look like. I'd like to know if I have any biological brothers and sisters and other relatives. It would kill off a bit of curiosity I have about them."

Helen thought that "It wouldn't make a lot of difference but it would satisfy my curiosity. If I never met them it wouldn't bother me a lot. It would bother me, say ten percent, but if I met them I wouldn't regret meeting them. It would satisfy me. A lot of it is curiosity: what they look like, who they are, who I look like, who I take after. I'd also like to know my grandparents. I've never really known my [adoptive] grandparents. They both live [in Europe]. I only met them twice. And I'd just like to know who my grandparents are. I'd like to know what they're like compared to my parents, compared to me."

Suzanne joined the majority. "I'd be happier. I have all this curiosity built up about them."

Lena repeated Suzanne's general ideas. "It would give me a history. Let me see where I came from. Satisfy a curiosity."

Rhea had met her birth mother a year earlier, when she was seventeen. She told me about the impact it had made on her. "It was like this big, huge, ultimate question was answered. It was being able to look in the mirror and being able to identify with someone."

In answering the question, "What would you do if your birth parents came knocking on your door?" Suzanne, the fourteen-year-old whose adoptive father had abused her, was the only one who was willing to consider a parenting relationship with her birth parents. No one else wanted to try to fit their birth parents into his or her life as some kind of parent-substitute. Many thought their birth parents might be friends, or friends of the family.

Cindy-Lou explained, "I wouldn't go away from my [adoptive] mother, but I'd try to be a friend to my birth mother. I guess I'd try."

Lena said, "I think I'd like my birth mother as a friend. Someone who could be a buddy and come over for coffee."

Nicole was more cautious. "If we got along I'd try to treat her as a friend of the family."

Stevie was blunt. "How should I know? They might be idiots."

Sherry said, "It would be hard to do that [fit birth parents into her life] because they'd be no different from any other friend. They were never there in the beginning. It would be really hard to fit them in."

Sarah said, "I'd respect her as a friend, I think. But my *real* mom and dad are the ones I have. I think I'd like to see my birth mother now and then. But not yet."

Rhea, who knew her birth mother, told me that she considered her birth mother "Fifty-fifty as a friend and as a kind of a mother. She can't really be my mom. She wasn't there to change my diapers. She wasn't there to make me feel better and wipe off the tears. But now she's there to talk to when I need someone to talk to and I can't do that with my adoptive mom because she is just such a judgemental person . . . . I tried to find my [birth] mom when I was fifteen and being bounced from foster home to foster home. Everyone kept saying, 'You can't find her until you're eighteen' and I kept saying, 'I don't need her when I'm eighteen, I need her now!' I found her when I was seventeen and I'm glad I did. But like I said, she wasn't there in the beginning for all those years and she didn't 'mother' me. She's a friend, though."

Mike had a little trouble telling me exactly how he felt. "Maybe I'd fit them into my life as friends. I sure wouldn't kick out my mom and dad, if my real mom showed up. They put me up for adoption, so . . . .This could all be different if I was adopted when I was older. I'd have different feelings about my [birth] parents then. I might have liked them. Or they might have abused me and then I wouldn't like them. I don't know them at all. I don't know if I would want to know them."

Leslie said that she would talk to her birth parents. "I feel resentment toward my birth mother. Why couldn't she have kept me? But I've spent nineteen years without her and I've turned out pretty good." Debbie thought it would be difficult to fit her birth parents into her life. "I don't think I'd want to. I mean, I have enough problems as it is. I think a lot of problems would arise from any relationship like that too. Sue [foster mother] has motherly feelings toward me. She's only seven years older than I am, but still, she has motherly feelings toward me. And my [adoptive] mother! She'd be really threatened by it. But Sue would understand. She knows I would never leave here to live with either of my parents. I've reassured her so many times. We've had a lot of discussions about that one.

"Those two [Debbie's foster parents] would do anything to make me happy. They'd bend over backwards for me, and they have. But I'd do the same for them. Other people would be affected if I started a relationship with my birth mother. It would even affect my relationship with my boyfriend. He thinks it's an excellent idea that I want to look for her, but then again he'd probably get upset if I had any more demands on my emotions." Debbie had looked at how she was handling her life and decided that she could not, at this time, juggle any more relationships, including one with a birth mother.

Helen thought that her birth mother would "never be a parent, but it would be nice to have her as a friend. I was really upset when I was about thirteen. I wanted to meet my birth mother then. My [adoptive] mom talked to me. She did try [to find her birth mother]. That helped me the most. My [adoptive] mom cared enough to try and help me go through the pain that I was going through then. I used to see those television shows like 'Little House on the Prairie' where they made adopted kids seem sad, pitiful. Like who was going to take care of them? That got to me. Probably I just wanted to be hugged by Mom, but I thought I really did want to know more about my birth mother."

Some adopted teens feel threatened by a prospective meeting with their birth mother. Does meeting their birth mother mean their adoptive mother is less "mom"? If their adoptive mother helps them search, does this mean she wants to give them up? While they may intellectually understand that their adoptive mother is trying to do her best for them, they may not be emotionally ready to accept this. Everyone who loves and supports an adopted child needs to respect his feelings, including the adoptee himself.

I asked Helen if she thought it would have been good to meet her birth parents when she was going through such a bad time at thirteen.

"No. I would have thought of Mom as Mom and my natural mother as a friend, but I probably would have done a lot of things wrong. Now I'd be able to handle it, you know, and talk to her. When I was younger I would have wanted to go with her. And I'd have regretted it now."

Judy, fourteen, who had told me at one point that knowing about her birth parents would be good because she might want to go and live with them, answered the question, "How would you fit your birth parents into your life?" with a defensive, "I'd meet them, but I want to live with my [adoptive] parents. I'd treat my birth parents as friends, but that's all."

The question is perhaps too overwhelming to be answered easily. Birth mothers have been shrouded in secrecy in most adoptees' lives, and a reunion would need preparation, discussion, and an exploration of expectations and feelings. It would not be a casual, easily-accomplished meeting. Most teens are not prepared for it. They want to feel secure in their present families and not threatened by a new relationship.

Over time as I contemplated the teens' words, a surprising wave of positive emotion for adoptive parents washed over me. The teens' adopted families, good or bad, were their families. I realized that they saw their *relationship* with their adoptive parents as important. They talked about it, revelled in it, argued with it, fought it, and appreciated it. They felt surrounded by parental feeling, even saturated by it, but they still wanted to know where they came from, why they were given up, and who their first parents were. They knew where they were; they wanted to know where they had been.

How does being adopted affect teens relationships with society at large? As children, some teens had heard taunts from other six- or seven-year-olds that strongly impressed them. "You're adopted. You aren't real." Small children, even when they have been told that they "were born in another lady's tummy," are often shocked by the revelations of the playground. Their attitude toward adoption is often one of great curiosity coupled with peculiar interpretations of their own. Years ago, when my oldest son was tiny, I had a state visit from a six-year-old neighbour.

"Mrs. Crook," she said, looking puzzled and avidly curious, "my mother says that your little boy is going to be a doctor. How can you know?"

I stirred that question around in my mind and finally said, "I think your mother said that my little boy is adopted."

Her face cleared. "that's it!" Then, "What's adopted? Isn't that some kind of doctor?"

The worst comments about adoption have come from adoptive parents (in very few cases) and from junior high school friends and acquaintances who seem to use the knowledge as a mallet. Teens told me that no one else seemed to care. If they were treated as a child with special status at home because they were adopted, this could come as a rude shock.

Some teens weren't particularly sensitive to taunts about adoption and suffered very little from them. When I asked Barry how he reacted to teasing in junior high, he said he couldn't remember because he wasn't really interested in adoption at the time.

Other thirteen- and fourteen-year-olds are particularly sensitive. Debbie told me that her older brothers always teased her. "They used to bug me about it. 'Oh, yeah. You were the ugliest one there. Our parents felt sorry for you so they adopted you.' I used to hear things like that all the time. I believed it. I trusted my brothers. They were sometimes nice, and when they were, I just thought the world of them, at least until about last summer when I found out what kind of life they lead—drugs and alcohol. Really screwed up."

Joanne was not harassed in her family, but she heard taunts from her "friends" in junior high school. "I'd hear, 'You were given up. You were ugly. No one wanted you.'" While Joanne understood that she was wanted in her family and that the teenagers were only looking for ways to be offensive, it still hurt.

Roberta, at nineteen, remembers how she suffered when she was fourteen. "I remember being called a bastard. I remember kids at school saying, 'Those aren't your real mom and dad. that's not really your grandma and grandpa.' When they said that about my mom and dad I was almost afraid that they were right. But when they said that about my grandmother I *knew* they were wrong. My grandmother thought I was wonderful. And my grandmother was *mine*. I remember the kids saying things like, 'Why would someone give their kid up for adoption?' 'Oh well, adopted kids have learning problems. They don't have the same feelings as everyone else.' I started to wonder if I was normal! I couldn't talk to my mom and dad about it. I mean, you lie so much to your parents when you're younger. You can't tell them how you feel. They have these expectations of the perfect daughter and you don't want to let them see any different. I had to grow up and they had to grow up and accept me."

Some adoptees feel that they must be the "perfect" child, that they must try very hard to fulfill their parents' and society's expectations. Such children may be the passive, compliant ones who act out only occasionally, but who bury their questions, anger, and insecurities deep in their emotional core, only to surface in later relationships. A quiet, compliant child needs as much information and discussion about adoption as the child who acts out.

Some parents tell their adopted children that they are "special" and "chosen." These labels often mean that the child feels he or she has to be exceptional. Because being exceptional is difficult if not impossible, the adopted child feels inadequate, never quite good enough. Compounding this is the notion that if he wasn't good enough for his first mother, he can't be for the second one, either. It would help to talk about this pressure to be perfect, but often teens don't understand why they feel inadequate and think that there is something intrinsically wrong with them.

Maryann commented on the vulgar curiosity she saw in the world around her. "A lot of people feel you're not really a person. that's their attitude. They want to know how you deal with being given up." She naturally resented being questioned like this.

I hadn't realized that there was even that much notice paid to the fact that teens were adopted. Many people have peculiar ideas about birth parents. There is still the expectation, as Rhea said, "That I'd find my natural mother in the gutter." Many people—adoptive parents, social workers, adopted children, and uninvolved observers—still believe that a birth mother comes from an unloving, unfit family, and lives in poverty, and that birth fathers are uncaring. This attitude persists even in the people whose sister or aunt or neighbour placed a child for adoption.

John, in his prosaic and practical way, gave a more positive view. "Usually you're put up for adoption because your biological parents can't support you properly and they want something better for you. Your adoptive parents want you."

Leslie was optimistic even though she was still arguing with her (adoptive) mother about her need to search. "I feel positive because I know a lot of kids who were adopted and didn't get along with their parents and couldn't handle the situation. They ended up going from foster home to foster home, or group home to group home, or group home to lock-up. They ended up getting pregnant at fifteen and giving up a kid for adoption, somehow getting back at the whole process. So I feel good that I had a good home; I was lucky."

Helen had similar feelings about her family. "When you are

adopted you can lead a normal life, a normal family life. Someone cared enough to put me out for adoption when they couldn't afford to keep me. They wanted me to have a good home. I've always seen adoption as a positive thing. I've never been mad at my birth parents. . . . I understand that a sixteen-year-old couldn't keep a baby—not really very well."

If the reason for relinquishing a child to adoption is most often the lack of financial support, and if poverty engenders ill health and few choices, then it's reasonable to assume that children raised in poverty would have problems. They are not genetically programmed for trouble. Statistically, adopted children fare better in the areas of crime and mental health than the children of their biological families, so to some extent being adopted into a secure home protects them from problems.

Judy, fourteen, viewed the parenting situation as a giant lottery—getting a good set of parents was purely a matter of luck. "Some parents are mean. If you search and find your natural parents, you might not believe they really are yours and they might not live up to your ideas of them. The best thing about adoption and living with your adoptive parents is that you get a real family."

I don't want to leave the impression that teens are constantly being questioned or put down by their peers. The incidents these teens described were isolated, but notable to them. Generally, teens didn't find many people who gave their adoptive status much thought. When I asked if they thought that being adopted affected their lives, they told me that it didn't really make much difference to them and that it definitely wouldn't make any difference in their future. Even when it obviously had influenced some during their junior high school years, they didn't expect it to affect them in their adult lives. And, even when the adoptees were a different race than their adoptive parents and/or brothers and sisters, teens still told me that adoption didn't make any difference in the way they fit into society.

Considering the number of adoptees who search for their birth parents and who feel that they cannot settle into their lives until they find their birth mothers, this view of the future may be unrealistic. Being adopted matters—they need to think about it, decide how they feel about it, and understand how society's attitudes affect their lives—past, present, and future.

Parents

What motivates people to bring a stranger's child into their home? Do they love all children, or anybody's child, or just this one? Are they concerned, loving people who want to give a child a home, or selfish self-serving people who want the appearance of the perfect family? Or are they complex combinations of all these needs and motives?

The need to adopt a child seemed simple and straight-forward. When I talked to social workers and parents, and when I examined my own situation, it was obviously more complex. Many times teens told me that their adoptive mother couldn't have children. "My mom has some kind of a problem and she couldn't have kids and they wanted kids, so they adopted." Sometimes parents wanted to be sure of the gender. "My mom and dad wanted a boy," or, "My mom and dad wanted a girl."

A social worker once told me that parents should make sure that they aren't adopting a child to show their families, their neighbours, and society how kind and generous they are; that they aren't using the child to improve their own social status. At first, I thought his suggestion ridiculous, but the more I considered it, the more I realized some people might feel that adoption was expected of them. Some religious groups encourage their members to adopt children in order to bring them up in their faith and give social prestige to those who do so. But even in situations where the motive for adoption is not just a matter of giving and receiving love, the children are most often loved for themselves. Reassuring us, researchers tell us that in over eighty percent of adoptions, parents and child remain together. It is difficult for anyone not to love the child who becomes part of his or her life.

Many couples adopt a child after a frustrating effort to conceive, and so may approach the adoption process with unresolved feelings of loss. While childless couples-by-choice are more socially accepted today than in the '70s or '80s, married couples were expected to have children at the time when today's teens were babies. This social expectation added pressure to those who had to face the fact of infertility. When parents are diagnosed as infertile, they often feel loss and regret for the children that might have been. This sense of loss needs to be resolved before adoption so that the newly adopted child doesn't become the obvious proof of the parents' "failure" to have "one of their own." The societal attitude that biological families are better than families that are blended with adopted children and stepchildren still exists. There is no reason behind this, other than the historical property rights argument, that is, the biological child as "rightful heir," but this attitude still operates in our lives. It helps to know that it is only an opinion and not a truth.

As a guest lecturer at an adoptive parents meeting, I was asked, "What do you say when your daughter looks right at you and says, 'You're not my real mom?'" The question startled me.

Such a question didn't seem a big problem, so I answered, "When that happened to me, I said 'Tough, kid. I'm the one you're stuck with.' The child is, in the time-honoured way of all children, only trying to upset you where she thinks you are vulnerable. You are, after all, *not* her real mother in that you are not her biological mother. You are her real mother in legal and emotional terms."

There had been a lot of emotion behind that question, and I knew that I hadn't really satisfied the woman. Much later, I realized that I had been denying the difference between a biological family and an adoptive family and had been anxious to downplay the question. In conversation with the social worker after the meeting, I asked why he thought the woman had been so upset by her daughter's question.

"I think the mother may have unresolved infertility issues," he said. "You have already had a biological child. 'Real' has a different definition for you. You can compare your feelings for your adopted and biological children and know securely that you love both intensely and that they love you. She is afraid that she doesn't love enough or loves too much or in some way is not a good enough mother."

We are all, at times, afraid we are not "good enough" parents. In fact we *know* we aren't good enough. It might have helped that woman to talk to other parents, to find that her feelings were common—as I realized when I was asked that same question again and again. On the other hand, although feelings of inadequacy are common, I don't want to minimize the power of the emotions around infertility.

Parents who feel threatened by this question may need to talk with a counsellor. Some researchers believe that infertility issues play out in the parents' attitudes toward the adopted child, and can be particularly deep and damaging in the father-child relationship. They believe that fathers with unresolved infertility issues are more critical of their adopted children and that they are more critical of their sons than their daughters. Parents might find it helpful to talk about this with someone who has experience with this problem. The reason a father is so critical of his son might have nothing to do with the son, and everything to do with infertility issues of the father.

Adoptive parents are often young—in their twenties or early thirties—when they adopt and often are not wise in their understanding of psychology. Growing up and understanding ourselves takes a lifetime. When we are young, new parents, we may not completely understand our motives.

With a stepdaughter and one biological daughter and unable to have more babies, I still wanted another. We felt our family was too small and we wanted boys. It seemed really quite simple at the time—it was about emotional needs, not reasons. I know that, until our last son was born, I felt our family wasn't complete. I don't think I looked any deeper than that. In both cases we waited nine months from the time we applied for our sons to the time they were born, so the whole process seemed quite normal. Other than a brief visit by a social worker, we weren't involved in a detailed home study, physical tests, or years of waiting. Although we attended a series of six pre-adoption classes, we didn't go through any serious introspection or examination of our motives for adopting. At the time, I believed that the pre-adoption classes were just another way for the social workers to evaluate our suitability as parents.

Many parents want a baby without examining their reasons. There may be many reasons and most parents probably have more than one. Some couples believe a baby will hold their marriage together or that it will make them feel more important, and more secure. Others believe a baby might make up for the faults of an older child, or that one with special problems will need them. Some may believe that adopting a baby will reverse their infertility and allow them to have a biological child. And some may not know why they want to adopt.

Kerri invited me into the house where she was babysitting. She was just nineteen and planned to go back and finish high school and then attend a child-care program at the community college as soon as she could. In the meantime, she supported herself with some help from her parents. Kerri was bright and pleasant, trying to find subjects she and I could talk about. She wanted to know and like me, and wanted me to understand her. She told me about her struggles to be independent at sixteen; how she wanted to live apart from her family, wanted to see them only occasionally, wanted to know her own mind, and trust herself. But these were struggles to become a separate person, something she had in common with other teenagers, not struggles against her adoption, or with the idea of being adopted. Now she lives easily and happily in her parents' home and feels like an adult who is accepted and loved.

Kerri told me of her understanding of why her parents adopted her. "Another lady was taking care of me and my mom went to see me and I was lying in this buggy. I was six months old when my mother found me. If she hadn't taken me I'd have died of pneumonia. I had pneumonia then. I lived in a buggy—that was my crib . . . playpen . . . bed . . . everything. I never had any exercise. Every time I cried, I guess the foster parents fed me. That's all they did. To shut me up they just fed me a bottle of milk or a cookie or something. So my mom saw me and she just said, 'You poor little thing. You come to me.' Like, my mom had two boys and two more boys she'd adopted and she'd always wanted a little girl, so she got me. I guess she wanted the experience of having a daughter."

As a young child, Kerri slept in a bedroom above the family living room. Her parents were unaware that she could hear, from her bed, every word they said below her. That was how she discovered that she and her brothers were adopted. It was exciting and special information that she immediately shared with her brothers. Their parents then talked about adoption with them and the subject has been easy to discuss since. Kerri doesn't feel any great need to find her birth parents. She's thought about searching and talked to her brothers about it, but she has decided not to look. She feels happy, secure, and loved by her family and boyfriend and doesn't see any need to disturb that.

Kerri spoke about her first conversation about adoption. "Mom and Dad sat us down all together and explained it to us. It felt odd at first. We all felt really strange and really different and we didn't know if we should tell our friends. We thought people are going to say, 'Ha ha! You're so ugly your mother didn't like you!' But as we grew older and I told my friends about it, a lot of them said that they would like to be adopted because then they'd *know* that someone really wanted them. And that's how I feel, and that's how my brothers feel, too, that our parents really want us. Up to about grade five I thought my brothers and I were the only ones who were adopted and it felt really good when we realized that other kids were adopted, too. . . . You think you are the only one—but you're not."

Kerri had the security of four older brothers, two of whom were also in the position of having been adopted into the family. She knew she wasn't the only one, or even one of the few who were adopted. An only child, or the only adopted one in the family, would find it more difficult to understand Kerri's perspective.

Some researchers think that adopted children who have non-adopted sisters or brothers have a more difficult time during adolescence. This may be worse if the parents had a biolgocial child *after* the adopted one. If parents had other adopted children—as in Kerri's family—the adopted child had an easier time during the teen years. The adopted child may feel reassured by another adopted child and threatened by a biological one.

Four teens I interviewed had sisters and brothers who were much older. Paul explained, "My parents already had raised my brother and sister and they thought they'd like to do it again, so they adopted my sister and me." In one case the baby replaced another child. "My parents had a son who died. They heard I was available, so they picked me up." Dan seemed to think that gave him a ready-made place in the family. Dan was also the youngest in his family. My own sons are the youngest as well.

There were also teenagers who couldn't remember why they were adopted. Fourteen-year-old Judy didn't think it was important to know why. "Mom told me, but I can't remember."

Reasons for adoption can be complicated. Adoption is not a fairy tale. Parents who may not know their own motives for adopting may find that the adopted baby does not provide the "cure" for their problems, or does not meet their emotional needs.

In two cases social workers placed children with families who were not ready to love them. As in all professions, not every worker is excellent. Some make mistakes. Some are beginners or are overworked, and others don't have the education needed to make the appropriate decisions for their clients.

I drove an hour into the suburbs to talk to Dora. She was alone in her boarding house in a well-kept suburb of a small city. Dora was eighteen and living with support from the welfare department, her income supplemented by babysitting and occasional jobs. She had dark hair, dark eyes, and a low, melodious voice. She had a logical measured way of speaking, saying what she meant thoughtfully and carefully.

Dora knew her birth mother had been young and unable to care for her, but she did not know where she had lived before she was placed for adoption at six months. Her adoptive father was a professional man who was away much of the time and her adoptive mother, while home with her, was unable to love her. At twelve years of age, Dora faced her mother's indifference and had to learn, after years of painful and unsuccessful effort, that she couldn't change the situation, that she had not caused it, and that her mother's rejection was not Dora's fault. that's a tough emotional fact that some adults never face.

I had a lot of admiration for Dora. By the time she was four-teen, she knew she could never be loved at home. She was placed in a good foster home with a loving foster mother until she was seventeen. Psychiatric counselling helped her to accept the situation. Now a mature eighteen, she seemed calm and stable, and although she blamed her parents, she also felt sorry for them. Her adoption was an unlucky deal. She was dealt parents who couldn't love her—that's the way the cards fell, that's the hand she had to play in life.

At seventeen, when her foster mother was ill, a different social worker placed Dora back home. Not a good decision. There she endured physical and emotional abuse for eight months before she moved to a boarding home. Dora wanted to work in Early Childhood Education, planing to help children have a better childhood than she did. She was as a survivor who was not looking back for a reason to fail.

It had taken years for her to understand why her adoptive mother couldn't love her. She had thought it might all stem from why she was adopted in the first place. "My mom had five miscarriages. Then they adopted a girl who died of a heart condition, then they adopted my brother, then two girls. One died of a respiratory problem and the other had cerebral palsy and they put her in an institution. And then they adopted me."

It was difficult to believe that one family could be subjected to such heartache. But it is possible that the other children were placed in temporary care as foster children. That might be why so many different placements were made.

"At that point, as far as I'm concerned, my mother's mental health must have been all downhill. The social worker couldn't see that. She never re-evaluated the home. She just went on her first assessment way back and never saw what it took from my parents to have all these children come in and out of their lives. By that time I think my mother was afraid to love any baby; she just froze. . . . my mom told me that the reason she never really got close was so that, if I left or something happened to me, it wouldn't hurt her." It was the circumstances of her placement, her parents' reasons for adoption, that made the relationship so difficult.

I asked if she thought it was a self-fulfilling prophecy.

"Yeah," Dora responded. "Bonding never really started. My family really broke apart when I was twelve. I've been in and out of foster homes since I was fifteen.

"My mother told me that my birth mother was raped. She said I was a rapist's child and that was why I had no heart and no feelings. And I believed that. It wasn't until I got my non-identifying information that I found out that my birth parents had been going together for a year and a half." Her voice hardened as she held back the pain. "Well, Mom, it was a really long rape; it was a year and a half."

The hair rose on my arms and the muscles of my neck stiffened. I was suddenly furiously angry at her adoptive mother. As a public health nurse I had seen children subjected to cruelty, neglect, and even persecution, but I have never accepted it. It always makes me angry. I reminded myself that I was only supposed to record Dora's feelings, not my own. The silence lengthened.

Finally I said, "Well, you know . . . that's a *cruel* thing for a mother to say."

Dora sighed. "I guess so. When I asked her why she had told me that I was a rapist's child, she said that my mother was fifteen and my father was eighteen, so it was statutory rape. Like legal rape. My mom knew they had been going together for a year and a half. She only told me that to hurt me.

"She upset me for a long time, though. I was trying to make some sense of life and going to school and all that, but I didn't think there were any feelings in me or for me at home. But I got help. My English teacher sent me to the doctor and he sent me to a counsellor. I went for three years because I was really disturbed. It really bothered me—that my mom didn't love me. After two years of counselling the psychiatrist tried to tell my mother what the problem was and she wouldn't listen. She walked out. I tried to get reunited for a year after that, but the psychiatrist said to give it up and try to shape my own life without them. The last time I saw them was two years ago. I was asked, more or less, not to contact them."

I asked her if she knew why her parents had wanted children.

"It's the little dream they had—the mother and the father. So it was the dream of having a little boy and a little girl and dressing them up and having a family and making everything complete."

Dora's story was difficult, but her moral courage was inspiring.

Sarah, nineteen and indulged by loving parents, had almost a fairy-tale experience. She told the story of her parents' expectations with pride. "My mom and dad couldn't have children and they wanted them really bad. They had a nursery set up for two years before they got me." Sarah was happily married now and still fondly attached to her parents. So many teens had had difficult lives that I was relieved and pleased to talk to someone who had had a happy childhood.

Lena also had good feelings for her parents. She felt they had conducted a search for her. They had needs around race, and Lena satisfied them. "My parents wanted a baby that had one white parent and one black parent—like them. They waited for a woman to have this baby and the baby turned out to be blonde and blue-eyed. They said, 'No way.' So they looked around until they found a baby that had black skin, and that was me."

Lena felt that she had met her parents' requirements and so was entitled to her position as a daughter.

The reasons why parents adopt are varied, but the parents of the majority of teens I interviewed truly wanted a child at the time of adoption. Almost uniformly the parents were middle-to-high-income earners. None of the teens had been adopted into a poor family; none had ever worried about getting enough to eat. All of them, including those of mixed race and those who didn't know what race they were, felt that they belonged in the social group they lived in. When parents adopted a child, the child in turn adopted parents, the family, and the community in which they lived. All the teens I interviewed felt a strong sense of identity with their group, family, and community. "I wouldn't want to be anywhere else," seventeen-year-old Nicole said. "I mean, I don't want different friends or a different school or a different family. Nothing else would be mine." This feeling could be part of being a teenager and may change as they grow older. Race and biological heritage, as with non-adopted people, matters more when adopted children are in their twenties and thirties.

There were two exceptions to the teens' feeling of entitlement to their families and communities.

Suzanne, age fourteen, wanted another chance with another family. "I'm not loved here. Something else, some other home, might be better. I don't get along with my mother. My mother has unreasonable rules, not normal rules. I hardly get along with either of my parents. They sort of treat me like a stranger—like I'm not really theirs. They treat my brothers [biological children] like angels. Maybe my birth mother might want to see me."

I interviewed Suzanne at the beginning of this project. She had an unhappy family situation and was especially sad since she could see no future there. I had talked to her mother first and had been told all that was wrong with Suzanne. The implication was that the mother had done her best with Suzanne and failed, so there was nothing more she could do. At fourteen? Just when a girl needs her mother? Suzanne's problems seemed deeper than the usual "Mom is so ignorant" attitude that is common to thirteen- and fourteen-year-olds. I felt a great sense of sorrow from Suzanne.

Several years later, Suzanne called to ask if I could give her a copy of our taped interview because her psychiatrist thought the interview might help her work on her past. She told me at this time that her adoptive father had been sexually abusing her. "I wanted to tell you when you interviewed me. I started to a couple of times," she said, "but my mother was in the house and I was afraid she'd hear me."

I had sensed her unhappiness, but had not known its cause.

Not everyone had a happy family life. An important question seems to be whether teens felt wanted now—whether they felt loved, respected, and valued now—not what their parents' reasons for adoption were in the past. Some had a clear understanding of why their parents had adopted them, for good reasons or bad; some had no idea. But, with the exception of Dora, who looked to the parents' reasons for adopting as the site of her problems, most showed little interest. More important was the way the parents treated them now.

In spite of the teens' insistence that their parents' reasons for adoption were not important—fourteen years can seem eons away for teens—those reasons still cause behaviours and reactions in the life of the family. Parents' lack of awareness of the reasons they had wanted to adopt may interfere with their relationship with their adopted child. They may find themselves in patterns of thought and behaviour which are detrimental to loving relationships.

There are many ways in which motives for and unspoken beliefs about adoption make the relationship between parents and children, particularly teens, difficult. Consulting a psychologist or counsellor could help both to understand what is involved in that relationship.

Adoptive parents often consider the effects of heredity on their child before they adopt, and periodically throughout the child's life, especially when the child is in trouble. In the peace and love years of the '60s and into the '70s, some parents believed that children only needed love to become "as if born to" the family. Today, we are more aware of the way in which heredity influences our children.

Heredity is the curly hair the birth mother gave the baby, the gender his father gave him, the allergies, blue eyes, long fingers. Heredity is black skin, slanted eyes, a small nose. What he is when he is newborn *does* make a difference. It matters that she was born a girl and programmed to become a tall woman with excellent health. Her life would be different if she had been programmed to become a short man who suffered from allergies. It might not be better or worse, but it would be different. It matters if a child is born a boy with brown skin into a society that still equates skin colour with character traits and political ideals. Heredity was not as important, the teens told me, as how they are treated, what their family is like, and where they live. But still, heredity is an important factor and parents very often consider it so. No one I interviewed had a parent who claimed that the positive characteristics of their child was a result of environment and the negatives a result of heredity, but it may be an unspoken belief of many.

Sometimes adoptive parents tell children about only the positive aspects of their heredity. Cindy-Lou was thirteen years old, a precise and organized thinker. I interviewed her in her suburban home; her mother welcomed me, then disappeared into the back of the house while Cindy-Lou and I talked.

Cindy-Lou knew quite a lot about her birth parents—what they looked like, ethnic background, talents—and she tried to incorporate what she knew about her past into her present life: "My mother liked to play the guitar and piano and sing. She's just like me." Cindy-Lou believed that environment affected her life about sixty-five percent and heredity about thirty-five, but she still wanted to identify with her biological background. "When I'm eighteen I want to try and find them [birth parents] and just meet them and stuff. . . . See what they're like. I've always wanted to meet them. Do they have any other children now? It won't make any difference to my life, really. It'll just satisfy my curiosity. I don't know how to go about finding them, but I'd love to do it. I'll ask my [adoptive] mom to help." Cindy-Lou saw her adoption into her particular home, school community, and neighbourhood, as a gift given to her by her birth mother. "I'm not any more special or any less special because I'm adopted. I'm just like other kids. Kids don't believe this 'very special bit.' Maybe I'm a little bit spoiled. My friends say I'm a bit spoiled." Cindy-Lou seemed to accept her heredity, but then she knew quite a bit about it.

The question of heredity is a fascinating one. A baby comes with genes that are programed for specific talents, body appearance, disease, perhaps even character traits. I've alway thought it the job of parents to encourage the good traits and discourage the bad. It didn't make much difference to me if the undeveloped combination that came in a baby was from my background or not. I have enough peculiar relatives in my history to keep me from being too sanctimonious. But I believed that it was part of my job as a mother to teach my children how to develop their talents. When my father-in-law told me that my three-year-old son kept time to the music because "Indians had a natural rhythm," I almost hit him. I'd spent three years singing to the kid; he had his own record player and records; I held him up to the piano as soon as he could depress the keys. While I was willing to admit that he might have arrived with the germ of musical talent, I refuse to think that I wasn't part of its development.

I had expected some teens to ask about their ancestors several generations back, but none did. While they were avidly curious about their birth mother, they didn't care very much about searching further back into their pasts. They seemed anxious to establish themselves into a normal, biological, family *one* generation back. Not that they wanted to live with that family; they just wanted to know where they began. They wanted their original history to give them a sense of belonging to the human race; to feel that their thread of life connected with the fabric of everyone's life. Charlie was ironic. "I mean, I'd like to know for sure that I didn't come off a tree or something. Did I come into the world normally the way everyone else did?" Intellectually, he knows he did, but emotionally, he doesn't always believe it. Some adopted children feel it disloyal to their adoptive parents to inquire too closely into their biological family. Adoptive parents need to make such inquiries more possible and comfortable.

Paul was dark, energetic, friendly, and keenly interested in the whole concept of adoption. He took a lunch break from his work as a hairdresser and we did the interview in my parked van on the street. He was nineteen, the youngest of four children, and seemed secure in the love of his adoptive parents. His brother had offered him a good opportunity in his beauty salon, and Paul was enthusiastic about his future there. Paul's parents were a hard-working older couple—the father was of retirement age, the mother fourteen years younger. He felt a strong sense of belonging in his family, in his religious community (Baha'i), and in his town.

Paul knew that his birth mother had kept him with her for about nine months and then finally placed him for adoption. He'd been told that he was in and out of ten foster homes before his adoptive parents took him at age twenty-two months, but he had no idea why he'd been passed around so much as an infant. Living on his own now, he got along well with his family. He saw his childhood as average, stable, with petty little differences with his parents that didn't seem important now. His parents gave him advice and encouragement when he asked for it. Paul was financially independent, but the family definitely felt a moral responsibility toward him, and he to them. The family is of mixed race—Paul and one sister appear to be aboriginal; his older sister is white, her husband, black.

Although he was curious about his birth mother, Paul was not willing to risk his secure family ties just to satisfy his curiosity. His ambitions were not centred on his beginnings, but on his future. He planed to be a hair stylist—a good one—"world famous."

Paul, like so many others, would like to know more about himself. "I mean, a little ethnic history would be nice," he said. "Am I

Native Indian, Italian, or what? I don't have a clue. I should know that. My future *children* should know that. I look different from my brothers. A month ago I realized that I'm not like everyone else. That I'm not a white guy. At least, I don't think I'm a white guy. It was just so weird. The only way I see it as different is physically different. . . . I really noticed it this summer because after the first two weeks in the sun I'm black like a berry. So it's strange. But I don't consider myself mentally or culturally different. I've even pulled out my I.D. to prove I'm my brother's brother. But, as a matter of fact, I look like my two sisters [one is adopted, one is a biological child of his parents]. We all look alike. Really dark hair, dark eyes, dark skin. But my brother [a biological child] is the one that looks different."

Others had similar problems concerning race. Bill told me, "I don't know if I'm sort of Chinese, or Indian, or what. No one knows. No one's telling *me* anyway. I'd like to know where I came from even if my parents were running drugs. It would be better than not knowing."

Like many teens, Bill thought that if his parents had been "good people" he would have some information and that no information meant they were "bad." This assumption is one of adoptive parents as well, but it is not true. Many adoption agencies just did not record accurate information.

Some parents believe that they cannot influence their child's development, that the child who was most often illegitimate was somehow the repository of all the genetic faults from both sides of the biological family. In spite of the fact that a look backwards in time into their own histories will reveal both wonderful and pathetic characters, some adoptive parents believe that legitimacy protects biological children from inheriting the "bad" traits. They have concerns that mental illness and criminal behaviour is inherited, and more likely inherited from poor people, as birth parents are assumed to be. Parents may have read studies that discussed the emotional and physical problem of adopted children and attributed those difficulties to heredity.

Studies tend to ignore the many strengths of adopted teens. Teens often have a strong belief in their own resilience and faith in their own individual personality. Stevie was just such a person. We met in a shopping mall in a city—her choice. She had wanted to meet without her parents' knowledge—probably her usual mode of running her life. She was cool and blunt, did a few drugs (she said), found school too easy, and thought her parents played roles. I was impressed, and a little startled. Thin and dark, she spoke in short, clipped sentences with a habit of freezing suddenly when I was speaking, as if I had said something fascinating. Her eyes twinkled whenever she found my questions and her own answers entertaining. The joke wasn't shared between us, but she enjoyed herself. She was a determined, and very intelligent, young woman.

The youngest of four adopted children in her family—two brothers and a sister came before her—she talked about adoption as an accident of birth and of little importance now. Adoption was "no big deal" to her. Stevie felt strongly that she had a right to her adoptive parents' attention and support, and that her position in the family was secure, although her parents could have done a better job of raising her. Her complaints were about methods of child-raising and not physical or emotional abuse. A drawback of her intelligence was her perception that she was more capable than most people and certainly more capable than her parents. Although she knew they would help her with her future, she was quite able to manage her own life. She made me nervous. I wasn't that confident at forty.

"As far as adoption goes, it's no big thing. Usually if I say I'm adopted, and if it is something big to the person I'm talking to, they don't believe me anyway. A bad thing is from all those crazy anti-abortionists that say if you don't want the kid, put it up for adoption. I think that's stupid. What's the point of going through a pregnancy and then giving it up? But then, if you're a parent and you want a kid, I guess adoption would be good for you. I mean if there wasn't adoption, you'd be stuck, wouldn't you?" Adoption to Stevie was a valid legal process and a person who was adopted had, like anyone else, a real place in the family. Any other attitude was melodramatic.

Stevie had definite ideas about heredity and environment. "Well, where you live is one hundred percent. that's the most important. How you look? I suppose some people like blondes, right? If you wanted to hire a blonde instead of brunette? Well, I guess it would matter some. If you're a woman instead of a man, I guess that affects you about fifty percent."

With her quick wit and strong opinions about her place in the world, Stevie reminded me that while teens can share developmental tasks and difficulties, they are individuals who react in their own way to the challenges of their lives. It was inspiring to realize that while adopted children share common fears and patterns of behaviour, as do adoptive parents, everyone is capable of individual unique responses.

The teens I interviewed were, for the most part, not concerned with their parents' reasons for adopting. In spite of the fact that those reasons might still be an underlying and important factor in the family dynamics and relationships, the teens saw the reasons as ancient history and not part of their lives.

No matter how a child comes into the family—through adoption, as stepchildren in a marriage, or by birth—they cause a change in the family constellation. Imagine two planets moving in orbit, each spinning in its regular pattern of movement, passing and repassing each other. Add a third planet with its own pattern of movement, and then a fourth. The relationships of each to the other are compounded and the possibilities of collision increased. If the parents had no children before they adopted, the change seems almost overwhelming. If they had other children, they may not have prepared for the ways in which children and childhood needs not only interact in their lives but engulf them, occupying most of their time. This change is one that all families make and may not be much different for families of adopted children, although the reasons for creating this change in adoptive families might be different. Generally, adoptive parents plan for the child, and parents of biological children are sometimes surprised by a pregnancy. One man I talked to, a teacher, had experienced an unplanned adoption. He was approached by a former student who asked if he and his wife would adopt her baby. They had only a few weeks preparation time before the baby was with them. Most adoptive parents don't have babies suddenly dropped into their arms.

Once the baby is in the home, the changes that occur to the family seem to be similar—feeding schedules, colic, baby showers, immunizations, and the ongoing activities of childhood—whether the child is adopted or not. Parents want to be part of their children's lives and, since they are the caretakers of their child, they must be part of their lives.

Parents may have many fears about the process of adoption that they don't discuss, either because they don't recognize them, or because of feelings of loyalty toward their children. They may fear that heredity is stronger than environment and that their child's heredity is faulty.

Parents of adopted children sometimes fear that the child will reject them because they are not "real." This, as indicated earlier, could be a result of parents' concerns about infertility, or it could be a feeling of lack of entitlement—that they are not good enough, rich enough, mature enough, or capable enough. When parents have other biological children, they find it easier to believe that these feelings are common to all parents, and that parenting is a difficult and often humbling experience in which few feel capable or deserving.

Parents also, especially in the first few years, worry that the birth mother will take their child away, or that the courts will return the child to a member of his or her birth family. This happens rarely, but that is enough to make most parents fear it, if not actively or with daily apprehension, at least with an underlying niggling worry. Many adoptive parents have heard of the birth mother who, when the child is eight months or a year old, decides to sue for custody, and wins. Adoptive parents are less likely to remember when the birth mother or father sued for custody and lost. No wonder adoptive parents aren't sure of their entitlement, when the courts occasionally decide that they are somehow *not* entitled to their adopted child. When the child is a teen, this fear is less a threat.

All parents at times fear that they are not good enough parents. But adoptive parents are concerned that they are somehow missing that bond, that intuitive knowledge that they think biological parents have. As Karen said, "I felt a natural mother had a certain touch with her own child—like she kind of knew things about her own child." Parents sometimes feel that their child's birth parents might have understood him or her better. It takes years for some adoptive parents to realize that their child isn't looking for the perfect parents and just wants a relationship with the nurturing ones he has.

Adoptive parents most often believe that they have more financial resources than the birth parents because, after all, lack of money is probably the most common reason for relinquishing a child. However, I once did a television show in Toronto with a birth mother, adoptee, and adoptive parent where the birth mother was much more educated and wealthier than the adoptive parents. Usually, adoptive parents do have more financial resources. In any case, adoptive parents generally do not feel they lack the ability to care for their child financially.

Parents often don't want their child to stand out as different from the rest of the family. Instead of seeing difference as something to celebrate, they may see it as threatening and refuse to talk about it or even acknowledge it. Should adoptive parents point out the differences between the child and others in the family and talk about them as a positive thing? Emphasis on difference can result in children feeling that they don't belong in the family. Should parents pretend that there are no differences? These are not easy questions. Obvious physical difference such as skin colour, or other physical differences such as a short boy in a family of giants, can lead to feelings of alienation. It seems reasonable to assume that parents who discuss these differences and listen to their child's views in a receptive, positive way, will help their child accept himself as a person who is entitled to his place in society with confidence.

Sometimes parents fear the surprise of a child's talents and career choices. Adoptive parents treat their children "as if born to," and expect them to fit into the family's class and modes of behaviour and to have similar educational accomplishments. Thus they are dismayed when the children choose different paths. Studies have shown that adopted children generally achieve less education that their adoptive parents. We can speculate on why this is so, but it is probably not because they have less educational opportunity. If the children have low self-esteem and are preoccupied with thoughts of rejection and "not belonging" as they reach the teen years, they may not be emotionally ready to study and make the gains in education that their adoptive parents expect. As well, they may not feel entitled to a higher education, a better job, a "good life." It is a parent's responsibility to set expectations for their child and to help that child to achieve the moral, educational, and social development that are necessary to lead a happy life. Sometimes the child's low self-esteem makes those expectation impossible; sometimes it is the expectations that are impossible.

Society

When I speak of North American society, that vast land of millions of people, I realize that there are many different cultures. And within the many different cultures are different attitudes toward adoption. North American "culture," the one in which most people live and understand their lives within the milieu of a modern, fast-moving world of television commercials, pop music, and changing fashions, contains mini-cultures—the small towns, isolated villages, French settlements, Mennonite towns, Mormon communities, street people, and the hundreds of other smaller cultures. "Society" and "culture" are vague terms and it is impossible to state definitively what any society or culture thinks or believes. Not only are their many societies, they are in constant motion, in a continual process of change. With these restrictions in mind, we can perhaps try to understand society as the imaginary larger force in our lives into which we fit into roles as mother, father, businessperson, teacher, doctor, mechanic, son, daughter, friend, and lover. It is this world in which we live that influences us and motivates us. Some people have a spiritual life that is also rich, interesting, and influential, but even that spiritual life exists within the society, and is even shaped by it. By "culture" and "society" I mean the everyday lives of most people, not the rich, famous, or literary. Given the limitations of the word "society," I trust the reader to imagine a definition that makes sense and is useful.

How does the process of adoption work within our society? We have evolved from the era of secrecy of the 1940s to the 1960s, with its notion that the child was "as if born to" the family, to the general acceptance, at least among professional adoption placement agencies, that the child's biological history should be preserved. This represents a significant social shift from the attitude that denying there was any difference between a biological child and an adopted child meant parents were noble, to the other extreme where celebrating differences by bringing attention to adoption is socially responsible. Birth mothers who gave up their children and promised never to look for them were considered noble once; now they are thought to be irresponsible. The actions haven't changed; the attitudes have.

In this book I speak of adoption as the legal process of making a stranger's child part of a family. There are many adoptions where a stepparent adopts his spouse's child; aunts, uncles, and grandparents adopt their relatives. Those children adopted by relatives may know their family histories, although there can be secrecy and deception around those adoptions as well. All but two of the teens I interviewed had been adopted at birth, but there are many children adopted after infancy. Their memories and their concerns may be different from the teens interviewed here. The definitions of both open and closed adoptions differ according to the agencies, birth parents, and adoptive parents involved. Some adoptive parents are willing to exchange information with the birth mother at the time the child is born and send pictures for a few months, and then perhaps yearly. The birth mother is not the legal guardian, nor is she expected to nurture and sustain the child, but to maintain a distant interest or a "watching brief" so that she is continually reassured that the child is being well-cared for. The purpose of open adoption is not to allow the birth mother the chance to direct and influence the child's life, but to give her to feel enough at ease about the child's situation that she can get on with her own life. The difficulty for some adoptive parents is that when a birth mother remains in their child's life, however distant, they cannot pretend that he was born to them and are forced to acknowledge that the adoption process is different from the biological process. This reality is hard for some adoptive parents who have been socialized to believe the "as if born to" myth. An adoptive relationship is no less strong a relationship than a biological one, and perhaps that is what parents need to be reassured about. The first time someone criticizes your adopted child and you have an enraged she-bear reaction, you realize that the maternal or paternal bond is powerful.

Birth parents give up the right to their child and can't, on some future day, claim the child. At fifteen, Mike had not known this. "They gave me up. that's done. They don't have the right to take me back, do they?" he had asked. He was relieved when I assured him that they didn't. It is highly unlikely that a teen who has lived all his life with his adoptive family would be ordered back by the courts.

The Adoption Act in all provinces and states makes the adopted child the child of the adoptive parents for all purposes. This means that they are children of their adoptive parents under all laws, can expect the same rights and privileges as a biological child, and can inherit equally with biological children. The law removes any legal differences between biological children and adopted children, making them legally the same. The Adoption Act, a provincial act in Canada and a state act in the U.S., establishes that the adopted child is a legal child of the family, a status that is binding everywhere.

This doesn't mean that people don't argue in court and try to change the laws. Occasionally, people demand rights that the law doesn't presently grant them. Sometimes adopted kids are surrendered to the court as "incorrigible," or unmanageable, in the same way that biological children are sometimes handed over to social services when parents can't cope. But most often, adopted children stay with their adopted parents for their lifetime.

The adoption process, the way babies are placed for adoption, is not simple and straightforward in all parts of the continent. Each province or state has its own rules, policies, and practices. Some religious and political organizations have their own adoption agencies so that they can place the children of their members within their own group. Some agencies accept babies whose mothers belong to a certain religious denomination or racial group and place the babies within the same group. Other agencies accept the baby of any mother and place it into homes that are culturally and racially different.

In private adoptions, the child is usually in the home when the social worker's assessment visit is made. While the law requires the visit, the worker would need valid grounds for apprehension in order to remove the child. In spite of some bad publicity, private adoptions are not necessarily poor adoptions. Adoption, after all, began as a private initiative. Large private systems, such as Catholic Charities, have been placing children in homes for years. Children adopted by aunts and uncles, stepfathers and stepmothers, and by neighbours, are usually adopted privately. North American society is seeing more and more private adoptions as the waiting list for government adoption agency placements stretches in some cities from months into years. Parents are travelling to foreign lands to find babies, and the legal and ethical concerns around adoption are growing.

Even when a placement agency sends only Catholic babies to Catholic homes or aboriginal babies to aboriginal homes, the needs of the child are usually very important. Even if they restrict themselves to one group of babies, the motives of the adopting parents may be loving and accepting. As well, the parents who adopt from religious or private agencies don't necessarily reflect the ideals of the placement agency, although they may be chosen because the agency thinks they do. Sometimes parents agree to an organization's policies only to adopt a child. Once the child is legally part of their family, the parents may not follow the philosophy advocated by the adopting organization.

The intent of government agencies is first to serve the best interests of the child, then the birth mother, and finally, the interests of the adopting parents. While that is the philosophy, in practice some government workers can be incompetent and/or overwhelmed with work. If the best interests of the child are to be served, then the child would most often be placed in a family that already has children, has been proven stable, and has had years of practice raising children. Because it seems more equitable to adopting parents to place children in families with no children or only one child, and as such families are in a position to complain about the service they aren't getting from the agency, the first choice of most agencies is to place a child with child-less couples, or those couples with only one child.

Social workers shuffle adoptive homes in what seems to be a capricious game of chance, juggling the needs of the child and the needs of adoptive parents with estimates of how long they think the marriage of the adoptive parents might last. The lucky winner gets a baby. In fact, there is a careful system in most agencies. Adopting parents are selected by the social worker and birth mother to match, as closely as possible, the religious, academic, and socio-cultural background of the birth mother. One knowledgeable and experienced social worker told me that the most successful matches occur when the birth mother thinks the description of the adopting parents sounds like a description of her family. But more and more families are accepting difference as a value they want in their family, and adopting across racial and cultural lines. Some birth mothers choose to have their child adopted by a different-race parent.

There are birth mothers who are pressured into relinquishing their child. Kendra, now twenty years old, gave a child up for adoption four years ago. "The social worker told me that if I wanted to keep my baby I'd have to do it on my own; the welfare wouldn't help me. She told me it was illegal for me to get welfare and to hurry up and decide." In fact, the policy of the welfare department of her province was to support the mother if she wanted to keep the child. Kendra had very bad luck in the assignment of her social worker.

"I couldn't make a quick decision. I wanted to look over the files of adopting homes really carefully, so I put my baby in foster care for two weeks while I read the files and tried to decide. The social worker told me to hurry, that they had a problem getting homes and that I had to pick one of the four she offered me. I insisted on seeing more files. The social worker told me that my baby was screaming all the time and I had to hurry to get her into a good home. I was totally honest with the social worker, and she lied to me. I have a real grudge against social workers now. I never saw that worker again after she placed my baby. I wanted to be left alone when I was pregnant and no one would leave me alone. And then after, when I needed someone, they all left me alone.

"I wanted to write a letter to the parents when my baby was six months old, but the social worker said they didn't want to hear from me, to 'forget it.' She hung up the phone on me.

"The social worker would do things like keep me waiting in the office. I'd have a one p.m. appointment and she would be across the street eating lunch; I could *see* her and she'd keep me waiting until two. She treated me that way, maybe, to make me feel inadequate so I'd give up the baby easier. My social worker specialized in adoption.

"The father of the baby offered to help me. He offered me money and he offered to marry me. But a kid is no basis for marriage, so I didn't want that. And my mother was strange. She and my father were divorced and she had some funny ideas. I was afraid that she'd charge the father of my baby with rape because I was only sixteen, so I wouldn't tell anyone who he was."

The strongest check on all social agencies on the placement of a baby comes from the birth mother. If she demands that a certain order of priority be followed in placing her child, the child is more likely to achieve a good home. But most birth mothers, like Kendra, are young and emotionally vulnerable right after their delivery. It's hard to be strong when you are physically tired from childbirth and emotionally distressed at parting with your child. Some birth mothers have parents who harass them. It's hard, immediately after childbirth, to make the right decision.

Occasionally, the birth mother has not signed a release and her child can't be placed for legal adoption. In these cases, a child may go to foster care and then occasionally be forgotten in the bureaucracy of the welfare office. Some agencies now have a system of tracking in place which should prevent children from disappearing between papers in the welfare office. There seems to be no system of legal checks and balances that forces social workers to do their best to find homes for children. Rather, it is a moral and professional obligation which is strongly felt by most social workers.

My family had wonderful social workers when we were looking for our sons. They were competent and caring, each with a sense of humour. I had worked with many social workers when I was a public health nurse and had met a few who were less than competent, but only one that was uncaring. The stories the teens told me about the pressures they received from social workers and the uncaring attitudes came as a shock.

Children in Canada who are given a status number as a First Nations person are in the position of having the federal Indian Act take precedence over the provincial Adoption Act. In the U.S., Native American children do not receive a status number, but they are enrolled in a tribe, either with land under a treaty, or without. In both countries, what they gain by being registered as an Indian under the Indian Act can't be taken away by the Adoption Act. So children who are members of a First Nations or Native American nation don't lose their identity when they are adopted. They are legally adopted, but still have status as a Native Indian. This means that they have not only the rights of a legal child within their family, but also the rights of a Native Indian in Canada or the U.S.

In Canada, children in this situation have the right to apply to the tribal band in which they were registered for funds for post-secondary education, medical care, and other services. They can also apply to live on reserve and ask the band for any reasonable help with their lives. At the age of twenty-one, they can choose to be a part of the band, or to accept a financial settlement. The band could vote to refuse such a settlement to a child, but it is unlikely. Rules and regulations can change, however, so this could be different in time.

Aboriginal adopted children who travel to their Reserve or Reservation may meet a warm, friendly group of relatives, as my son did, and find that they have a place in the clan system. On the other hand, the family may not be interested in them or may be suspicious of their motives for "returning," and reject them. Aboriginal children will need the support of their adoptive family and a trusted counsellor in either case. Both acceptance or rejection can be very emotional.

Occasionally, a band may decide that a child born of a band member who is not registered as a status Indian may have the right to band funds. In the U.S., Native American children have the right to the benefits of treaty if they are enrolled with a tribe that has treaty benefits, as well as rights to health benefits, education, and welfare. If they are without a treaty, they have rights to health, education, and welfare only. What rights a biological family decides these children are entitled to is neither legislated nor predictable. Adopted aboriginal children may need to meet their biological family to find out if they will get support.

Many First Nations and Native American organizations have departments that help adoptees find their birth parents and may even help pay travel costs. If adoptive parents cannot accept the teen's need to connect with the biological family, this search could be very difficult. It will be much easier with their support.

Native American teens in white families may feel as though they don't belong in either culture. Often they are viewed as "Indian" even if they have never lived in that culture, so they will be treated as if they grew up in Native culture. They may discover that being part of that culture is a source of strength. It also may be confusing and disorienting, a cause for emotional turmoil. Their race is an aspect of their life that they must understand and accept.

Racial differences don't seem to mean much when adopted children are teenagers, although it may become important later in their lives. None of the teens I interviewed concerned themselves with racial, religious, or political motives around adoption. They didn't see themselves as saviours of religion or race, and didn't see why they should involve themselves with anyone else's problems with adoption.

Andy and Allan, both fifteen and adopted from Korea at a young age, didn't think that cultural heritage was important. *Their* culture, they told me, was the teen culture they lived in now, not the culture they came from. They didn't see themselves as part of their Korean culture and didn't see why they should consider any other place in society, except within their family.

Karen said, "To an adopted child, adoption is personal. People who are not adopted . . . should not speak about it or judge it." Those teens I interviewed who were a different race from their adoptive parents felt that race as well as adoption was a private affair. The Caucasian sister of a First Nations teenager told me about the racial differences between her and her brother. "It never occurred to me until one day I was introducing my brother to someone and I suddenly thought that they might think it odd that we had different-coloured skin. Until that time I'd never thought about it. He was just that colour. Like I had blue eyes and he had brown. I was eighteen, and, hey, I'm pretty smart, but it was only then that I noticed we were different." While racial difference may affect adopted teens, they often do not believe it does.

Adoption often serves the best interests of the adoptive parents and the adopting agency. Over the years, many people have been concerned about the child's best interests, but concerned people make decisions with the knowledge they have at the time. Very often, the best interests of the child are not clear, or are mixed into the culture's notion that claiming a soul for a religion was in the child's best interest, or that sending a child so far away from his biological family that they could never connect was "safeguarding" the child. What one era views as beneficial, another era sees as cruel.

Amendments to the laws on adoption can be passed at any time. What seems to be written in stone one week can be changed the next. Lawmakers are responsive to lobbying by interested groups. Those who wish to change the adoption laws can write their member of the provincial legislature or state legislator about what they want done to make the laws better or more useful for them. Social workers must operate under the law—they can't give information if the law forbids it. To change what social workers do, you have to change the law.

There are some incidences of babies placed for private adoption in a system that seems to be buying and selling. Some countries where children are bought and sold don't regulate lawyers carefully. International adoption agencies can give advice on this. And in some countries where lawyers are regulated, there are still many who try to buy and sell babies. In an attempt to control this, some provinces and states have introduced laws such as the one in British Columbia (1980) whereby the law "prohibit[s] the offering or accepting of a consideration of value in money or in kind for the purposes of inducing a person to make a child available."

This law was tested in 1982 when a couple applied to the Supreme Court to allow them to pay the birth mother of their child some recompense for her expenses. The judge allowed the adopting parents to pay the travel, medical, and legal expenses of the mother. The courts didn't want to make recompense for medical and legal expenses unavailable to the birth mother; they only wanted to prevent the birth mother from benefiting from the transaction—to prevent the business of selling babies. Different states interpret similar laws differently. What may be a legally acceptable payment in one state may not be in another, but all U.S. states are making efforts to prevent trafficking in babies.

The Law Societies of most provinces and states frown on lawyers charging exorbitant fees for finding a baby for a client. The lawyer is supposed to arrange the legal adoption, not be a broker for the clients. Professional ethics should prevent baby brokering. Some lawyers who specialize in adoption help birth parents and adoptive parents come to agreements which may be perfectly legal and helpful, yet may come close to brokering. Any lawyer suspected of selling babies should be reported to the Law Society.

There are children who are brought from foreign countries for adoption in the United States and Canada. But all adoptions in the U.S. and Canada must come under the state and provincial laws, so if children were adopted in their country of origin, they will be re-adopted in their home state or province. If adopted internationally, children must have immigration status in the U.S. and Canada. An adopted child from a foreign country is not "automatically a U.S. citizen. Nor will the child automatically be admitted to the U.S. once adopted" (Bascombe, 1997). With many different levels of bureaucracy in the home country, foreign country, and in international laws, adoptive parents need the help and guidance of an adoption agency. Once children are legally adopted, after the order has been processed and passed, they have the same legal rights in their adoptive family. It makes no difference to the adoption order where they came from as long as the order is proclaimed in their new country. The adopted child becomes the child of the new family. An adoption order in one state or province is legal everywhere. While adopted teens feel the need to find connections to birth families, they also need to know that their connection to their adoptive family is strong, enduring, and legal.

The influences on teens around adoption are personal, familial, and societal. As teens grow, they move from the strengths of their adoptive family into society, and it is as they mature and take their place in that society that their attitudes to adoption, and the attitudes of those around them, make a difference in their lives.

Chapter 3

The Developmental Path

If I am in harmony with my family, that's success. -UTE SAYING

WHEN I ADOPTED MY SONS, I did not have an outline of the developmental stages that they would most likely travel. Other than the advice about telling my children they were adopted at an early age, I had no understanding of the fear of abandonment or issues of the disruption of bonding that can lead to trust and intimacy concerns of adopted children. We are only beginning to understand that adopted children have a normal and possibly predictive maturation path. Adopted children may have a developmental path that is usual for them, but different from someone who has not been adopted. The issues that are important to an adopted person don't magically resolve themselves. When an adoptee becomes a parent, he or she needs to have worked through many of these issues so that concerns around identity, belonging, and relationships aren't heaped upon the shoulders of their first baby.

Teens rarely have an opportunity to consult an adoption counsellor. There are few who specialize in teens and adoption, and they can be difficult to find and finance. Most counselling around adoption occurs at the time of placement. There is little ongoing or even periodic discussion about how being adopted makes a difference in the life of the adopted teen. Most teens don't have much experience of adoption except their own, and most parents don't either. That means that they don't have examples and mentors to help them adjust and cope with the unique family situation they find themselves in.

One of the most restricting and inhibiting notions about adopted children that parents have is that the child will develop as do non-adopted children, that the child will follow the same path to emotional maturity and self-acceptance that non-adopted children do. Adopted children are a specific group, with their own normal path of development. They need information, education, and experiences that are different from non-adopted children in order to move through the conflicts and challenges of their lives to maturity in a happy and satisfying way. Adopted children need connections, reassurance and a vision of a firm and defined position in their family and in society.

As well, in spite of the theories of Freud, Boult, and many other psychiatrists and psychologists, adopted children need to stay close to their adoptive mothers. It has been common in the past to believe that boys work through their Oedipal complexes in order to become men. This means that they must repudiate mother, and take their place with men. This societal pressure to "be a man" by rejecting not only mother but everything about himself that society views as "feminine" is intolerable for adopted boys. Girls are not required to reject their mothers. In fact, they are expected to love and care for their mothers their entire lives. The societal pressure on boys to distance themselves from their mothers in order to become masculine in their teen years creates a huge conflict within the adopted boy. If he successfully distances himself from his adoptive mother, he then has had two fundamental losses: his birth mother and his adopted mother. North Americans have a peculiar culture that makes rejection of mother a necessary component of manhood. Some psychiatrists say that this process of rejecting the mother is an innate psychic one that will occur without any social demands. Since other cultures do not have this process, it is likely that it is a socially constructed one that society has forced upon us and not one that comes from our need to be autonomous (Pinar, 1999). The very difficulty of the process, the tremendous psychic pain that this effort to separate causes, ought to alert us to the fact that such a separation is hardly good for anyone. It makes the confusion that adopted teen boys often experience much more understandable.

If adopted children have their own normal emotional maturation path, what do they need and when do they need it? No one has set this information out clearly with any validity so that adoptive parents can have a "manual" for raising their children. Following are some areas that cause adopted children great concern; parents need to find ways to deal with them. Awareness and anticipation of what most adopted children find difficult, will help parents plan for ways to help their children.

The teens I interviewed told me that they need information

about their birth mothers. This information should be given to them in a simple form when they are very young, but in more and more detail as they grow older. Adoptive parents worry about giving teens what they consider negative information—that their birth mother was in jail, for instance. Parents need to work on their own attitudes and try to present the information in a broad context. If a birth mother had been in jail when she gave birth, she is probably no longer in jail and, in any case, was no doubt leading a more complex life than just "being in jail" implied. When children ask about negative information, parents can relate it to their own family trees. It usually isn't hard to find less than perfect people in their own heritage; having disreputable relatives in the parents' lineage doesn't mean others in the lineage must be disreputable, too. Teens need to feel that parents have confidence in them as they are and that their chances of succeeding in life are good.

Ongoing conversations about adoption can be difficult to initiate. Adoptive parents often tell children that they are adopted when the child is four or five years old and then never refer to the subject again. It is important that adoption is presented as such an accepted practice that parents refer to it as it comes into their lives naturally—at the doctor's office when asked for a history, at school when heritage day requires a list of ancestors, when creating a family tree, and in the company of friends and family. Not talking about it again tells the child very clearly that it is a taboo subject, which makes it even harder for the child to accept. Conversely, if parents talk about adoption too often, children may believe that parents are uncomfortable with it, and even feel that they are constantly being reminded of their difference. How much discussion of adoption is helpful and at what ages is it helpful? There isn't a reliable answer. Telling the adoption story as truthfully as possible; engaging in conversation about it when the child asks questions; and initiating conversations about it occasionally are probably reasonable guidelines. It is important to be truthful, direct, and accepting. Having said that, I admit that talking about adoption seems to be an art form.

It is usually in the teen years that the feelings of loss and rejection that come with being adopted need to be faced. When teens begin to think about what it means to be adopted, they have to face the fact that they have suffered a loss. The ways in which parents and teens talk about this are crucial in helping teens to cope with it. Adopted teens face a few more developmental hurdles than their non-adopted friends.

It is very important that adopted children feel firmly connected to their adopted family and their extended family. grandparents, uncles, aunts, and cousins. These connections are what make lives rich and what allow adopted teens to feel firmly in place in society. Adopted children also need connections to their birth families. They need to know how they are woven into that family as well as into their adopted family. This need becomes stronger when the adopted child is a teen, or, for some children, when they are in their twenties or thirties.

While all children need reassurance that they are loved and wanted, adopted children need a great deal of reassurance throughout their childhood and adolescence. Their appetite for proof that their parents love them and will continue to love them may seem insatiable. Separations are difficult. The toddler who cries when parents leave becomes the eight-year-old child who is upset if parents are late picking her up from school, and grows into the teen who doesn't want to leave home, doesn't want to go away for a weekend, and insists on knowing where everyone in the family is at all times. It helps to talk to teens about this as normal for adopted children. Often parents understand their child's need for reassurance without realizing that it is common in adopted children. All children need reassurance, but adopted children may need it more.

The first abandonment, the day their birth mother relinquished them, is seen by some researchers as a trauma that affects adoptees profoundly because it happened before they had language to describe it. This "pre-language trauma" sparked a whole-body response of grief in the baby—an overwhelming sense of sadness which envelops the entire mind and body. According to the theory, from then on, when adoptees had issues of abandonment and loss—when their father leaves the family, when their hamster dies, when their girlfriend dumps them—they again experience a whole-body response. Instead of saying, "This loss in my life makes me sad," they responded with whole-body grief. There aren't proven studies to back this up, but it does seem to resonate in adoptees' lives. If there is truth in this, then adopted teens need to talk about their losses as they happen even more than other children do. They may have a great need for reassurance and understanding about loss. For adopted teens, fitting into their society and learning how to be independent and to have higher self-esteem may take more time and attention than for non-adopted teens.

Researchers talk about two reactions of children to adoption—the acting-out of aggression on the one hand, and passivity on the other. Verrier (1993) suggests that if there are two adopted children in the family, one will be aggressive and one will be passive. These behaviours seem to be a result of adopted children's belief that their adopted mothers will abandon them as did their birth mothers. Adopted children can have varying degrees of these behaviours as a reaction to their first separation from their birth mothers, or, as Sarah seems to have done, they can talk with their adoptive parents often and in detail about their feelings and manage to avoid either extreme.

Adoptive parents must be clear about what position each child in the family occupies. Biological children will jockey for position and settle into what works well without much direction or consideration by parents. Adopted children may need more direction in order to understand and feel confident in their position. It may feel tenuous to them, and so they may continually test it, striving for power in the family. Recognizing that adopted children need to feel important, a valued part of the family, and that this is often not easily attained, helps parents provide a definition of their position by saying something like, "Yes, I love you. You are my first child. You are the oldest. You are the one who first made us a family," or, "Yes, I love you. You are my youngest child. You are the one we were all able to lavish love on. You brought us all together and made our family so much more interesting and lively." It is important to be sincere, honest, and specific about why a child matters to your family.

Adopted children have already lost one mother. Somewhere in their emotional memory they suffer a great loss; they cannot tolerate losing another. Adoptive parents need to find ways to help their teens to become autonomous and independent without forcing them to separate from their adoptive mother before they are ready. As well, adoptive parents need to be more understanding about the role mothers play in the lives of their adopted children. This can be difficult, because teens who are having problems may react or act out through addictions and compulsive or anti-social behaviour. Rescuing and supporting teens so that they do not have to face the consequences of their actions does not help them. This, in the accurate parlance of Alcoholic Anonymous, is "enabling" the behaviour. If the teen has anti-social, harmful behaviour patterns, adoptive parents need professional counselling. Parents must be sure to find a counsellor who understands the profound effects of adoption so that the "tough love" directive that is often recommended is balanced with the adopted child's particular need for reassurance.

Health statistics show that adopted children are referred for mental health consultations more than non-adopted children. The reasons for this are not always clear. The behaviours of the children might warrant the referrals, or the families of the adopted children might be more likely to seek help. As well, parents might be more difficult to live with than biological parents. Are adopted children born with behaviour problems? Of course not. But they may have particular difficulties they must confront. This in no way implies that adopted people are sick because they are adopted, or that there is something about adoption which makes the children ill. What this implies is that adoptees have additional or different emotional paths to maturity and contentment and that it is in everyone's interest to try to understand this.

The problems of early abandonment, along with concerns about subsequent feelings of loss and low self-esteem, have not been studied well enough to reassure us that learning problems and criminal behaviour don't come with the adoption papers. Intellectually, we may know that adopted teens are responsible for their own actions and won't end up in jail or in suicide unless they choose anti-social behaviour but, emotionally, adoptees may fear that "being adopted" has made them less valuable and less worthy than others. Lower self-esteem leads adopted kids into trouble the same way it leads all kids into trouble.

A. Bandura (1963) and other researchers stress the importance of fathers in a child's development. Becoming an adult is more a socially learned process than a physically determined one. How we treat children and how we interact with them is more important than their hereditary tendencies. The teens I interviewed thought so, as do most adoptive parents. Adoptive parents, like others, may be tempted to give up on their child during the teen years. They may believe that they can make no difference in their child's life. That is not what the teens say; it is not what the educators say. When I interviewed teens for a book on suicide prevention, I found that twenty-seven out of thirty teens rated their relationship with their fathers as very low. The time when fathers are tempted to turn away from their teens, when they are convinced that they are not important or influential, is exactly the time that teens need fathers the most. Fathers, said the teens, are *very* important.

Adopted children have the same needs as non-adopted children to develop aspects of themselves in a progressive and maturing fashion. They need to develop a sense of trust, accomplishment, self-esteem. They need to feel they belong in their families, in their society. They need to make educational and occupational choices. Adoptive parents must understand that adopted children's normal developmental needs are compounded by their initial separation from their birth mothers and the sometimes complex attitudes and emotions within their adopted families. The needs of adoptive children are reasonable and normal. Adoptive parents can help them greatly if they understand this.

As teens move through adolescence into their twenties, they have the usual challenges of their age as well as issues around adoption. Like most people, adopted teens will deal with their age-related tasks the way others do, in a patchy and uneven manner, sometimes *not* dealing with issues that seem too difficult by pasting defences over them or moving around them. To establish themselves in intimate relationships and perhaps begin a family, adopted teens will need to deal with the usual concerns of all adolescents and develop physical competence and health, mental skills, and academic qualifications, a reliable spiritual core and emotional maturity and stability—the huge demands of a fulfilling life. In all the concerns of teens around emotional issues, some seem to stand out in the life of adopted teens as particularly difficult. The teens I interviewed were sometimes aware of the scope of the tasks ahead of them, but even when they were unaware, they usually revealed the same central issues as difficult for them. They had concerns around rejection, dependency, self-worth, and connections to others.

Adopted teens can look at their first placement in their adoptive home as a time of joy for the new family, a new beginning. At the same time they can see it as rejection by their birth mother, an ongoing sorrow in their lives. Even when a teens says, "My mother was too young and couldn't look after me, so she did the best she could by placing me in a good home," such an intellectual assessment may still translate in teens' bodies as emotional rejection. They may not be aware of this, yet operate from such a belief with compelling force and set up intimate relations with a built-in expectation that they will be rejected. Adoptive families are often well aware which child—and it isn't always the adopted child—is sensitive to rejection and try to reinforce love and support. It is not possible for parents to live their child's life for him, though, and rejection is part of life. People sometimes *are* rejected for one reason or another—it's a common human experience. Teens may need to work through this expectation of rejection so that they don't see it as an inevitable component of intimate relations. Not every relationship will end in rejection. It is possible to have a long-standing, happy, emotionally fulfilling relationship. It is difficult for parents to help here because, although they may intellectually understand the problems their child is having, the remedy is emotional and the child must travel through the process of accepting intimacy by himself.

Independence, both physical and emotional, is a task of teens and, in our North American culture, that can take a long time. We probably have the most prolonged adolescence humans have ever experienced. It is not uncommon for children to return home time and again until they are in their thirties. Friends tell me that their twenty-three-year-old son or their twenty-seven-year-old daughter has returned home to stay "for a while" during a job search, to recover from a failed marriage, or simply to save money to attend university. Living at home with Mom and Dad encourages feelings of dependency, and adopted people, like anyone in this situation, may find it difficult to become independent. But adoptees may need more reassurance that their parents love them even as parents ask them to leave home. Requests that children be independent do not mean that parents are rejecting them.

It takes maturity and experience to learn to trust that the world is a place which will accept and sustain us. Adopted teens must come to trust that they are entitled to the largesse of the universe, that they will find a secure place in the world. They need to be aware of how they fit in their culture so that they can live advantageously, and know that the culture will support them. This trust in the universe and its abundance is related to their own sense of worth and self-esteem. Parents may continually try to encourage their children's self-esteem, but during the teen years self-esteem is hard to maintain. In a world of successful movie stars, music-makers, and athletes, and with the constant parade on television of the young, rich, and famous, teens can feel that their "ordinary" lives are inadequate and their contributions to the world woeful. Parents can help by referring to the world around them, the real accomplishments that occur in small increments, and to the joy and contentment of an ordinary life.

During the teen years, a sense of ancestral continuance can help teens to feel at home in the world and entitled to a valued position within it. This is the time that information about their heritage is most helpful. That heritage doesn't have to be inflated. My own paternal ancestors were a very poor family living on a rock in the Outer Hebrides. They were not influential, rich, or financially successful. They just were. Yet I felt supported by a long line of tough, ordinary people. Teens need to know that they have a lineage, however ordinary, infamous, or nondescript their ancestors may have been. They need a sense of their place in the history of the world.

If teens have a solid and reliable sense of self-worth, if they see that they have a place in society and that they are loved and accepted, they can deal with the difficulties and tragedies of life in ways that help them grow. Spiritual strength comes from living through adversity. Adopted teens need to learn, the way all teens need to learn, what their options are when they make decisions, and they need to learn to live with their decisions. Parents must give teens space to make decisions and allow them to live with the consequences. Habits such as compulsive eating, lying, and escaping in sexual addiction and substance abuse are ways of avoiding difficult issues, and avoiding issues threatens teen development. Becoming an adult isn't simply a matter of time. One does not become emotionally mature and spiritually wise simply by getting older. Becoming an adult is a matter of decision-making and choices. Escape mechanisms only allow time to go by; they don't allow teens to grow.

Teens must understand that in order to become an adult, they don't have to be perfect or do everything perfectly. Learning means starting with incompetence and proceeding to more competence, not perfection. They will have their own timetable; experience takes time. They should be kind to themselves and give themselves time to become an adult.

It takes effort to keep relationships solid with one set of parents throughout these years. It takes a great deal of effort and emotional maturity to move through these years keeping positive relationships with adoptive parents, siblings, birth parents, boyfriends, and girlfriends. Teens need all the loving support they can find in their lives, and parents are usually their best source.

The teen years are a time of preparing for the future, a career. The pressure—even in very early grades—to choose a career path and assiduously and conscientiously study over many years to achieve it is daunting, and sometimes overwhelming. This emphasis on scholastic achievement also unbalances the teen's Medicine Wheel in that intellectual development and achievement is valued far beyond the emotional, spiritual, and physical. At a time when teens need to develop emotionally, there seems to be little space or support for them to do this. Counsellors and family members can help them look at choices and try to help them take their own time in creating a future. Teens must have faith in themselves. All the loving relations, all the parents, are needed at this time to support and guide teens. It is teens' task to establish themselves in the world, but they need to do this with all their loving and loyal relations.

Chapter 4

Search and Reunion

I MET BARRY IN THE CITY LIBRARY where he had spent the last two hours trying to track down a name in city directories. "Today's my day for Toronto and Saskatoon," he told me. "I have my mother's name, but since I was given up nineteen years ago, she probably married and changed her name, so I'm looking for her parents. I thought it would be easy, but I'm having a hard time finding any information at all."

Barry was good-looking, personable, and athletic. He spoke easily and confidently, an asset in his jobs as a salesman in a sport's shop in the winter and as a golf instructor in the summer. He lived in the suburbs with his adoptive parents and older brother, and seemed happy, stable, reasonable, and intelligent. Although he had always known that he was adopted, he hadn't been interested in it until this year, his "year for searching." The local Parent Finders Association had helped him, but he had received no help from social workers. He sees social workers as obstructive—looming like a standing army protecting government information. Barry understood that the social workers had to obey the law, so he sent letters of protest to his legislative representative asking that the laws be changed.

Barry and I ate our hamburgers and talked about the problems of searching for a past. He was curious and wanted the information, but he didn't feel that his life would be blighted if he never found it. His adoptive parents approved of his search, helping him get to started and encouraging him. Barry had no plans to live with his birth parents or get very involved in their lives, but he wanted to sit down and talk to them as if they were friends he hadn't seen in a long time.

He had given his reasons for searching quite a lot of thought. "It took me three or four months to decide to search. I started by phon-

109

ing the Zenith Child Line. The person who answered gave me the Parent Finders' number. So I phoned it one evening. I didn't know what was going to happen. I was really hopped up for it, and I was kind of nervous. The phone picked up, and it was a recording. What a let-down! So then I sent off a letter and I got more and more interested. The head of Parent Finders here isn't doing the search for me, but has given me a lot of advice. I got hold of the lawyer who did the adoption and he still had my adoption order. He didn't want to give it to me at first, but he finally did, and that's how I found my name."

Changing laws come from changing attitudes. This lawyer probably was reacting to the changing attitudes toward the adoptees' right to know their origins.

"I'm getting more and more interested in the search now. I asked the social workers for more non-identifying information and they wouldn't give me anything. To them it's not important. To me it is. I just want to know things like, was my grandfather Ukrainian? It seems kind of stupid to be against the law to find that out. I know they're try-ing to protect the birth parents; they don't want anything coming back. I tried to get information from the hospital because technically, for a couple of days, *I* was a patient. The administrator said, 'Well, we can't give you information in case the mother doesn't want you to know. She could file a suit against us.' I'm not sure that I couldn't file one too."

Today in Barry's province when adoptees ask the social worker for information, they should at least receive non-identifying informa-tion. More and more people are becoming aware of the need for con-nections, and information is not held back with the same kind of right-eousness as it was when Barry was searching. Not all states and provinces offer a co-operative attitude, though. Searching can still be difficult.

"I'm really curious about my birth parents and my background. I think it will be interesting to know. I've thought about whether my girlfriend would turn out to be my sister [if she had been adopted too], or if my dad is a famous rock star. It's all really far-fetched, but it's pos-sible. I look at my best friend and I think, '*He* knows who his parents are. What gives the government the right to keep my background from me?' From reading my non-identifying background I get some reasons for what I am, why I happen to have a certain colour of hair. And I play the piano. I took piano lessons for less than a year when I was twelve and I went through five books. It just seemed natural to me and it turns out that my birth father was a musician. He made his living playing in bands for a while."

I asked him how he got people to give him information. He spoke about being persuasive, a good selling tactic.

"You have to tell stories because you can't go out and just tell people why you're looking. People might decide, 'Oh, this was all hush-hush way back then' and decide not to tell you anything. And then they might go and warn other relatives not to tell you anything. I make up a kind of story, say I'm looking for an uncle or something. I know enough from my non-identifying information to get some facts straight. What happens if I have a twin or a sister or something? I don't have a sister now, just a brother. Discovering a sister like that would be kind of interesting and neat. I think about that every once in a while. I haven't put an ad in the paper yet. Every day I read the births, deaths, anniversaries, information wanted, and some of the personals."

After our one meeting, I never heard from Barry again. I expect that he did find his connections, because the law changed in his province shortly after our interview, establishing a reunion registry.

Some teens wanted to search for their birth fathers, but most wanted contact only with their birth mothers. I asked why. The answers were much the same—they wanted to know about themselves and their birth mother was their greatest source of information. They believed that their birth mother was the one person who could satisfy their curiosity and give them a personal history.

I was late for my appointment with Nicole at the fast food restaurant in the centre of Vancouver. She had left when I finally arrived. I called her on the phone and she came back to meet me. Nicole was seventeen, a student in high school, the youngest of two children; her older brother was not adopted.

By the time she was five, Nicole understood that she was adopted. As she grew up she became more interested, doing a report on adoption for her law class in high school. In doing the research for this she found, to her surprise, a negative attitude toward adoption in the books she read. Most were written by authors who had been adopted after infancy and who wanted to return to their birth parents. Nicole didn't share their feelings at all. She knew why she had been given up for adoption and was satisfied that her birth parents did the reasonable thing. Her birth mother and father had been engaged, but had decided not to get married. A month later, her birth mother found she was pregnant and chose to give Nicole to a two-parent family. Nicole would like to meet her some day to get some medical history because she doesn't think the "completely healthy" medical history she received was accurate.

Ambitious for her future, Nicole planned an academic career. Secure and happy where she was, she rated her parents a nine out of ten. But, in spite of her stability and optimism, she wanted to know who she had been.

She had mixed feelings about searching. "I wouldn't want to invade her [birth mother's] privacy. She might be living her own life, trying to block out what happened. It might have been a bad time in her life and I wouldn't want to bring it up again for her. I think I could accept that she might not want to see me. I don't think I would mind."

Many of the teens I interviewed were concerned that searching for their birth parents would hurt not their birth parents, but their adoptive parents. They recognized the need in themselves to have more information, perhaps even a meeting, but were reluctant to hurt the people they loved. "My dad would be threatened," Sarah told me, "even though I feel that my mom and dad are the ones I have, not the ones who conceived me. My [adoptive] mom would help me; in fact, she did help me. She saved all the information. She even peeked at the adoption papers when the social worker left her alone in the room. She remembered the information, including my birth mother's name, and gave it to me when I was fifteen. I didn't tell Dad, though. I don't think my mother told him either. He would be upset. So I have my birth mother's name and I looked it up in the telephone book. But I wouldn't phone her. That wouldn't be fair to her, don't you think? Maybe someday I'll get someone else, maybe a searching agency, to call her or find out if she wants to meet me. But not yet."

Many adoptive parents receive some papers containing "non-identifying history" at the time the baby is placed with them. This is a description of the birth parents and often their parents as well. It has been the policy of many agencies in many provinces and states to include racial origin, height of the parents, skin colouring, eye colour, any talents such as musical ability, and a medical history. It is a cold picture for many teens—as if they had been handed a file-card parent from a collection. Many teens don't have even this information. The adoptive parents may not have been given it, or they got it and didn't pass it on, or it may never have been taken in the first place.

Roberta was fair, pretty, and eager to talk to me about adoption. She lived with her parents and her seventeen- and seven-year-old brothers, neither of whom were adopted. Her family moved into the area, about an hour from Vancouver, when she was twelve. She had no friends at that time and felt unwanted. Previously a good student at school and an easy-going child at home, she became big trouble.

Roberta began lying to her parents all the time. And not only did she shoplift, but she became the leader of a group and planned shoplifting forays into the stores of the town so that the gang would think she was smart, daring, "cool." She did some drugs, left school, got work, was fired from her job. Then she got pregnant and told the father of the baby. He denied responsibility, so she told her parents she'd been raped. It was an overwhelming mess.

At fifteen she had her baby and placed him for adoption. She wrote him a letter telling him why she placed him for adoption and put her name in the reunion registry, making it as easy as possible for him to find her if he ever wants to. But she realizes that he may never want to.

"I wrote him and told him why I had to give him up. I told him how much I cared. For the ten days I stayed in the hospital with him, I was his mother. I fed him and washed him and looked after him. I'll always have that time with him and he had that time with me. *My* [birth] mother found me 'inconvenient.' She was thirty-one. See, there's no excuse. I was just inconvenient. I want to know how my birth mother felt. It's very, very hard to accept the fact that you were given up just because you didn't show up in time. You know 'Oh, well. Today's not convenient. We'll give you up today. If I'd had you a year from now, maybe I'd have kept you.' I find that hard."

And yet that is what had happened to Roberta. She had a baby at a time when she couldn't look after him, but her experience did *not* make her more understanding toward her birth mother.

I asked Roberta if it would have helped her to have met her birth mother at an earlier age.

"If I'd met my birth mother at thirteen it would be different from now. Maybe I'd have been looking for another mother then. Like I could have had two moms then instead of one. Instead of now, when I would be looking maybe for a friend and some answers. Now I've got my mom and I don't need another one and I don't want another one either.

"If I wanted to find her, I guess I could put an ad in the paper. Sometimes I'll see an ad that talks about someone born the same year as me, the same month, wrong day, and it kind of hurts. It's a boy not a girl, and I think, is that ever nice but . . . why couldn't she do that for me? I got the pamphlets {from a searching organization}, but they want so much money. . . ."

Roberta needed more information about the costs of a search. The cost varies; even passive registries may ask for a fee. When I inquired about what I had to do to find the birth mothers of my boys, the minimum fee for registration in my province was $25. A few years later when I asked, the fee was $50 to register passively, and $250 for an active search. For those with no money, the fee can be waived, but that means applying for and filing an income test and waiting for the application to be approved or disapproved. Roberta could have written or called searching agencies to ask about their types of search and how much they would cost, and whether or not she would qualify for a subsidy.

Years ago, people thought it was better if birth parents and adoptees never met. The purpose of the secrecy laws was to help make the adoptive family more homogenous. An adopted child was supposed to be absorbed into the family like the cream in a bottle of homogenized milk. Shake up the family and let there be no differences between adopted and natural children.

Agencies and lawyers did what they could to conscientiously assure that the birth parents had no way of finding the adopted child. In many provinces and states there were laws which prevented both adopted children and adults from searching for and finding their adoption orders. Previously in British Columbia, section fifteen of the Adoption Act read ". . . an adoption order is not subject to search. No person other than the Attorney General or a person authorized by him in writing, may have access to them; but the court, on an application . . . on good cause shown to the satisfaction of the court may permit . . . the applicant to inspect those documents. . . ." This meant that even adopted adults could not search for their birth name and parents without a court order.

Things are different today. In 1996, the laws changed to allow for much greater access to information. Section 19 of the new act reads, in part:

> (2) A person referred to in section 60 (1) of the Act may, on application to the director in the form and manner specified by the director, register on the post-adoption openness registry an interest in making an openness agreement to facilitate communication or establish a relationship.

Laws in provinces and states differ, operating from two perspectives. Either they are designed to make connections between all members of the adoption triangle easier, or they are designed to prevent those connections. Some provinces and states have access to information laws that let the adoptee look for birth parents, while some make that process very difficult. Current laws on adoption information sources are available on the Internet where the information on laws is listed by state and province. Or information can be found by writing to adoption reunion sources, some of which are listed at the back of this book.

The 1996 law in British Columbia provides a reunion service and ensures that access to information is much easier, except where the birth parent or the adoptee register an objection. Adopted adults may apply for their original birth certificate with their original name. As well, a birth father registry now exists where the birth father can provide information for the adopted child. There is also a post-adoption openness registry. Another program, a reunification program within First Nations or Native American communities, tries to find the birth parents of First Nations adoptees. Services are supposed to make the adopted adult's search for information and identity much easier. In some areas restrictive laws become redundant when adopting parents and birth parents exchange information before the adoption placement. In the future searching agencies and government registries will not be necessary because there will be no secrecy surrounding adoption.

Adoptive parents and birth parents are now more likely to feel the need to be open with and willing to celebrate the differences between them than in the past. Today, more and more adoptions involve a meeting between both sets of parents before the child is placed. If it occurs privately, the information exchanged is not subject to any provincial or state regulation. The agency may not arrange such a meeting, but may be willing to co-operate after the meeting has taken place. Perhaps the next generation of adopted children won't worry about their origins; they'll know who they are. More and more people now know that adopted children need to have their history and that the world will not hiccup and stagger off its path because they find their original parents.

Like Barry, most teens I interviewed were critical of social workers, so I called social workers to ask them what they were doing out there. What was causing so much hostility? I knew that obtaining birth information was the main frustration, so I asked workers in agencies from coast to coast about their policies and the rationale behind them.

Social workers in the planning departments of legislatures were desperately anxious to be effective, compassionate, and to act in the "best interest of the child." I was impressed by their intelligence, competence, and caring attitudes. For the most part they were supervisors of family services and probably not the workers teens would meet in the office. However, they were responsible for those workers and, in many cases, interpreted the policies for the social workers in the local offices. They were surrounded by legislation, public opinion, and individual lobbying, which made it difficult to respond with simple, compassionate solutions. It isn't possible to give out information if the legislature and government policies forbid it.

It was just as frustrating for some social workers to be prevented from acting in a simple, reasonable way as it is for teens to be denied their backgrounds. As with all laws, the ones that cause us a personal injustice are unfair, and anyone who obeys such unfair laws seems to be colluding with injustice. Social workers are aware of this attitude. Their only alternative is to ignore the law, betray their employer, and leave themselves open for lawsuits and breach of trust actions. It is not much of a choice.

Many teens had a poor opinion of the social welfare system. Dora said, "I don't trust social welfare. Social workers don't help. If my child had to go through what I did, I couldn't handle the guilt."

Rhea's birth mother told her, "I made a contract with social welfare to place you in a good home. When it didn't work out, why didn't they get in touch with me? They broke their contract. Why didn't they come back and ask me if I could help you?"

The system, while providing a chance at a good home, avoided telling the truth in a great conspiracy of information suppression. Teens also thought that the needs of the birth mother were ignored. Rhea didn't see why the birth mother couldn't have a periodic progress report from the adoptive parents on how her child was doing. As with most other adopted teens who were skeptical of the system, Dora was sure that a letter from the adoptive parents, given to social welfare and passed on to the birth mother, stood a good chance of never arriving.

Although many teens thought that their birth mothers had a right to information about their well-being, they didn't feel they had any right to contact them or interfere in their lives. They wanted the choice of whether to meet birth parents to be their own decision.

The Reunion Registry of Canada compiles statistics on those who are seeking information about adoption. At the time I checked, seventy-five percent were adopted children seeking information and only twenty-five percent were birth parents. So while teens see birth parents as having the right to knowledge about them, large numbers of them aren't asking. But we can't assume that birth mothers don't want to know their child. One told me, "When I signed the papers, I promised I wouldn't look." In trying to live up to her obligations, she didn't search.

Teens told me that the adoption-welfare system was "lousy." In some cases this was resentment about controlling and withholding information, and in others, it was an attitude that was the result of personal experience.

"The social worker put me in twelve foster homes before I was eight months old. I mean, what kind of a social worker would do that?" When I asked why she had so many homes, Karen said, "I don't know. You wouldn't get a straight answer from a social worker. Social workers are government. They say anything to cover themselves up."

Dora also was critical of the welfare system. "The way welfare works, you have a one-in-thirty chance of turning out okay if they're looking after you." Although Dora had some good experiences with social workers, her most recent experience had not been happy.

Bill was twenty-two years old, about five-feet ten-inches, dark, quiet, almost shy. He had a life-time of frustration with social workers.

We met over lunch and spent an hour talking about his life. He told me that he had never talked to anyone the way he was talking this day. I thought he might be Native Indian, perhaps part Chinese. He didn't know. His ignorance of his racial history was part of his problem.

Bill was in six or eight foster homes before he was six years old, then in an orphanage (he thinks). At eight he was placed for adoption. Apprehended by the court at from his adoptive parents' home age twelve, he then lived in several different group homes until he was nineteen. His adoptive parents had no history on him. The social workers told him they gave his history to his adoptive parents and now have no records. This is unusual. Copies are usually kept in the welfare office. Bill isn't sure where he was born, or even whether he is Canadian or American.

Although he was only with his adoptive parents for four years, he spoke of them as his parents and of his adoptive brother and sisters as his siblings. But he had only legal ties to his adoptive parents, brother, and sisters. He wanted to find his birth parents, not so much to establish a relationship as to establish a solid background for himself. He was afraid to develop any kind of relationship with anyone because he had suffered so much rejection. He knew this fear was a problem, but he didn't know how to handle it.

Bill trained as a cook and was working in a restaurant, and had ambitions to work in an even better restaurant. He has another ambition; some day, he would like to know who he is.

"I remember meeting my [adoptive] parents when I was about eight at the fountain. It must have been Vancouver, because I remember the Planetarium. I was apprehended from them by welfare when I was twelve. I remember going to court and sitting there from nine in the morning until two in the afternoon. No one told me what was happening. They just told me to be quiet and do as they said. They did tell me that my parents were charging me with 'unmanageability'. I knew I hadn't done anything wrong. But the social worker told me to keep quiet and just not say anything so they could get me out of that home. She said if I tried to tell anyone that I hadn't done anything they'd put me back with my parents, and I didn't want that." As a legal child of his adoptive parents, Bill could not have simply been returned to the social worker. He had to be apprehended or taken into custody in this case as a delinquent.

"I talked to my best friend later. His father, a policeman, thought my parents were treating me so bad that he reported them to welfare and that's why the welfare tried to help me. When I was older, I tried to get my background information and the social workers said they didn't have it. They have no records of me before I was eight. So they said. It's like it's okay with them; I didn't exist until I was eight.

"They put me in a couple of group homes and they were okay, but I never knew I was leaving a place until the day I had to go. Always on the day. I never had any warning. And they never did any follow-up. I saw my social worker once in the first year I was away from my parents. And then no social worker for three years. Any help I got, I got from the secretaries at the welfare office. Not from any social worker. No one talked to me.

"No one cared until I got a good group home. I had a really good group home from when I was fifteen to when I was nineteen—just great. Except for those group home parents, the social system has left me in a bad situation. I'm supposed to have dual citizenship because I was born in the States. I've lived in Canada since I was eight but, because my parents won't give me any information and because the social workers say they don't have any, I can't get Canadian citizenship. I've been here since I was at least eight! It's like I didn't really exist. I had the R.C.M.P. try to find out information and the Canadian Armed Forces try. I'm in the Reserve. They wouldn't let me into the active service because I couldn't prove my citizenship. But they just get a blank before I was eight.

"Everyone's pretending that before I was adopted at age eight, I just wasn't anywhere. I've tried to find out, but no one gave a damn and that's the truth."

Bill's need to know his origins was so reasonable and compelling that it is a huge injustice that society's rules deny him his information.

Some social workers have ethical problems when teens ask for information. They usually understand the teen's need to know, but have difficulty justifying the release of information because of conflicting loyalties to and past commitments of the agency. "We made a contract with birth parents and adopting parents eighteen years ago," one social worker told me. "We promised at that time not to reveal any identifying information. If we reveal the names now, we are breaking that contract and that's not ethical—no matter how much the child involved wants to know." This is a one point of view that keeps names and identifying information securely locked in the social workers' files. And it is a good point.

But this causes concern for some social workers. "Now, we [in Nova Scotia] try to get a letter from the birth mother and from the adopting parents authorizing us to reveal the name to the child, should that child ask for it in the future. We don't give the identifying information at birth, but we get a consent to release the information if asked by the child. That way we can actively search in later years if the child wants us to. We might not do that. The social worker would have to assess the situation and do the best thing for that time, but we will have more options than we have now." The information would still be released at the discretion of the social worker and would not automatically be given to the adopted child. But if the birth mother gave permission when the child was born, the social worker may be able to help when that child searches. "Adoptive parents and birth mothers could write in and change their consent to this information being released and we would have to respect that."

So, in spite of the very caring attitude that I felt from many social workers, the information they hold about searching adults who were adopted is controlled by the law of the state or province, and they will not release it.

In many cases the law causes a moral dilemma for the social worker. One worker from the Yukon Territory thought that the birth information belonged to the child, not to the welfare department, but she could not release the information to the child because the law would not allow her to. The Yukon had a passive registry at the time that held the birth mother's name if she had submitted it, and the child's information if he had submitted it. The social worker, in spite of her personal feeling that the child had the right to the information, had to keep the information secret until both parties agreed to share it. Now a birth mother can write to the social welfare department giving permission to release information to her child. As birth mothers become more aware of the problems their children are having trying to get information, perhaps more will write their permission.

The Northwest Territories of Canada is a land of vast tundra, awesome skies, and a society that reflects that space and freedom. It has a unique and practical adoption system.

When interviewing a worker in the Department of Social Services in Yellowknife, N.W.T., I asked her if children had difficulty in getting information about their birth parents. "Not really," she said. "We have a big area, but we don't have a lot of people up here and everyone either knows everybody or they can get to know them. Kids can find their parents if they want to. I've worked here for nineteen years and in this department for five-and-a-half, and it's only in the last year or so that I've been getting inquiries about birth information. I don't get many inquiries from teenagers who are searching, but if they have the permission of their adoptive parents, I help them. We don't have any legislation or any policies up here to prevent me from helping them. And it's really . . ." she hesitated, "it's really no big deal—no big secret. What's the matter down there? Do you have some kind of prejudice against adoption?"

She sounded so easy-going and reasonable that I wondered for a moment if we crazy southerners weren't making a big problem out of a simple matter. I asked her to tell me more about adoption procedures in the Territories.

"We have three different kinds of adoption. We have the department adoption which requires a medical, a waiting period, home studies, and then all that paperwork after placement. We have very few children that come into our care that way, so we don't have many adoptions processed. Then we have private adoptions. Most adoptions are done that way. Usually a child is given to a family by a mother who lives in the same community. The department worker does a home study and after six months, the adoptive parents make arrangements with a lawyer to process the adoption legally.

"The third way is the native-custom adoption which is pre-arranged with the mother. There is no six-month probationary period. The adoption goes through when the baby is placed in the home. Three documents are signed and the child becomes a child of that family by order. This is done sometimes when families exchange children, that is, a family with four girls and a family with four boys might exchange a child. While this is often workable, young mothers are sometimes pressured into giving up their child to a family they don't really approve of—like a pensioner couple. But it's fast and convenient and doesn't cost any lawyer's fees and it usually works out all right."

I asked her about the teenagers' need to search for their birth parents. "The only problems of identity that seem to come up are with the children who have been sent south. We didn't send many children south, but those who went sometimes come back to look at their old home. We try to keep all our children in the Territories."

"Do you have a policy of placing a child only with a family of his own race?" I asked.

"Well, now we don't have a real problem there either. The department has so few children to place that we try to get the best home for the child and that includes looking at his face. Most of the private adoptions involve relatives or people in the same community, so it's approved of by the community, more-or-less. The adopting parents approach the mother and ask her for the child. If she likes the home she'll put her baby there. It seems to work out pretty well."

I was impressed with the community solution to finding good homes for children—not a lot of official guidance, very little bureaucratic interference—just a community acceptance of parents' need for children and children's need for families.

"And because everyone knows who had the baby, it isn't hard for the child to find his natural parents if he wants to. I helped a sixteen-year-old girl last week find her natural mother. Her adoptive mother thought it would be a good idea, so she asked me to do it."

"How long did it take you?" I asked.

"Twenty-four hours."

It seemed ideal. I tried to imagine the social situation in New York State or Ontario if those governments implemented the adoption system of the Northwest Territories.

In many places there seems to be an attitude that the social worker must protect society from itself; that all parties to the adoption—the child, birth mother, birth father, adopting parents—must be organized and regulated by a social worker; that the parties involved could never reach a good decision without the professional advice of the adoption agency and its workers. In contrast, the attitude in the Northwest Territories seems to be that, if left alone with a minimum of interference, communities muddle through to a reasonably happy solution.

In many provinces and states, it is the policy of the welfare agencies that a child born in one city must be placed in another. If we changed that policy to approach that of the Northwest Territories, we might place a child in the community or city into which he was born. This would encourage more open adoption, similar to the policies of many aboriginal communities, and perhaps a more relaxed, reasonable attitude toward the child's beginnings.

In one sense, the intentions of lawmakers, social workers, and many adoptive parents to protect the child is wonderful. They are concerned that adopted children be given every chance to truly be a child of their new family. But the teens I interviewed didn't see the need for great secrecy. Adoption wasn't a social stigma, something to be hidden. The teens didn't view it as a problem. No one had been treated badly because they had been adopted and, except for incidences in junior high school, no one had encountered prejudice. Being adopted was not a social issue, although it may be a personal emotional one.

Some teens felt that they had been invited to the party of life holding a different colour invitation from everyone else; that they were only a temporary guest in life; that they might be asked to leave at any moment. This lack of background information, instead of unifying families, as the lawmakers and social workers had once predicted, caused feelings of alienation within families. In cases where adoptive parents helped their children find information about their origins, the teens felt closer to their parents—understood, loved, and appreciated. They felt their individuality was respected and accepted.

Barry didn't think that finding information about his background was important to anyone but himself. "I want to know about my background so I'm doing my own search. When you decide that you're going to search you have to be prepared to live with whatever you find. If you aren't ready to accept what you find, I don't think you should bother to search. You will have to accept the good or the bad, whichever way it turns out to be. After I find them I don't intend to change. I'm happy. I'm satisfied. I just want to know who they are."

Few teens knew the names of their birth parents. It may be that within ten years, most teens will have this information. In some provinces and states the names of the birth parents are given to the adoptive parents at the time of placement; in some areas the names are still kept secret. If teens have their birth name, finding birth parents may be easy. But most start with little or no information, so it takes ingenuity and persistence to trace their past.

Many provinces and states now have a birth registry. These differ one from another. Some are passive registries in which both the birth parents and the adoptee must register and are then "matched." Some registries are active, in which case, either the birth relatives or the adoptee may ask the agency to search for the other party. Some are "semi-active," in which case only the adult adoptee is helped in a search and the birth relatives will not be assisted. Some registries have so many applications for searches and so few staff members that they are seven to ten years behind in their work.

Some have registries for fathers; some allow family members to look. Some have veto provisions, which means that either birth parents or adoptees can refuse to allow contact or information to be released. And some provide that all identifying information that has been left with the agency will be given to the adoptee when he or she turns eighteen.

To be included on the registry, an adopted child must be an adult (usually eighteen, but some registries ask for adoptive parents' consent at eighteen and adoptees must wait until they are twenty-one without it). Searchers can write to their state or provincial government for information, or they can click onto the "Current Open Records Bills" on the Internet for up-to-date advice. Countries such as Great Britain, Israel, and Finland allow free access to the records to adopted adults. Since the records have become available in Britain, only a small percentage of adopted adults have looked up their backgrounds.

Laws change. Searchers might find information easier to access this year than last. Still, there is always the fear that information will be become more difficult to attain because of a backlash in some areas (the anti-open adoption movement in New Jersey, for instance).

There are many private registries that serve the adopted adult's need to find information. They offer advice and moral support, and suggest searching techniques. The Canadian Reunion Registry accepts names from all who wish to search. Again, searchers must be eighteen or their adopted parents must act for them. Those who wish to register must send their name, address, birth date, birth place, and time they were born. The registry fills out a card to keep on file awaiting the birth parent's information. The Reunion Registry ties into the American International Soundex Reunion Registry, which accepts searchers at eighteen years of age.

Registries on the Internet are organized according to province and state, and there is a World Wide Registry. Private registries started by interested searchers will often accept the adopted child's information, put it in a holding file, and ask them to wait until they reach eighteen. At the same time, they may offer advice and help. If an adoptee isn't comfortable with the first agency, he or she should not give up but try another. If adoptive parents apply on their child's behalf, some agencies will start a search.

There are several magazines devoted to the problems of adoptees. As well, the Web lists many searching agencies; some are volunteer, non-profit organizations; others are private, detective-like inquiry agents. With the opening of the adoption laws, it is less likely now that children or birth parents will have to hire a private detective to find each other. Many people find what they need to know from state or provincial records, or from reunion registries. If that does not get results, they can consult adoption reunion agencies.

My oldest son is not interested in searching for his birth parents. Every time I decide that he *ought* to search, and perhaps I should start the search for him, I remind myself that he is an adult, has told me that he doesn't want to search, and works as a private investigator for a living. If he wanted to find his birth parents, he could check all the sources I know about, and probably some I don't. It is important for adoptive parents to be open and helpful; it is also important for them to respect their child's opinions and desires.

A particular cultural background may be an advantage in searching, because sometimes cultural organizations keep records and may be able to help. Native Americans and First Nations people of Canada may have additional assistance because some nations have their own reunification departments which help people with a Native heritage.

The first place to start searching is at home. Adoptees should talk to their adoptive parents. They are the best source of information, often recalling facts that can be important leads in the search. They may remember bits of information the social worker gave them many years ago, or have a letter or a report filed away. Co-operative adoptive parents can be a great source of support and help. Often parents can find information quickly, and the process of looking for birth parents can bring adopted children and their adoptive parents closer together.

Leslie started looking for her birth mother when she was seventeen. "For me, it was hard because my parents were not supportive. My mother is very insecure. But she should have been a little more secure to know that, after nineteen years of her being my mother, I wasn't going to run off with someone who was . . . like a perfect stranger. She *should* have been supportive, but fear overcomes love there. Because they [my parents] were more afraid that I was going to find them [my birth parents] and want to go back there. I don't know why. But I suppose if I was a parent I would have that attitude, too.

"I couldn't talk to my mother because she got very upset . . . to the point she would phone me and somehow we would get into it and she would cry on the phone. All I wanted to do was know. And I'd gotten mad at her a few times because it had got to the point that it annoyed me that she would be that insecure. 'You're my mother. You're my father. that's all there is to it.' It's just that I want to know who they [birth parents] are; why they gave me away; what the circumstances were. My mom just had a really hard time handling it. Parents are better off supporting the child and helping her through it. Like a child is better off if she goes somewhere to meet her [birth] mother and her mother tells her, 'Well, I got pregnant and I was a hooker and I didn't want you.' Then you're better off to have your [adoptive] mother there to cry on."

Searching for a birth parent can be a time-consuming, frustrating process. If you have decided to search for your background, and you know your birth name, you might try to find information in the following ways. This information was obtained from the secretary of the Canadian Reunion Registry years ago, from adoptees who had successfully searched, and recently from the Internet.

1. Check the Internet. There are many different sites for you to search, most without fees. Type in "adoptee search" in the space in your search engine, and just keep hunting. I have heard that there are unscrupulous people who prey on your need to know and try to work on your emotions to extract money from you. The Internet is both wonderful and awful. Be careful about who gets your name and address, and check out the information you receive.

2. Check telephone directories (old telephone books in library

stacks.) Look for a father or brother of your birth mother. Male relatives are less likely to change their last names.

3. Check city directories showing residence, occupation, and full name. Main branches of libraries and archives may keep directories going back to 1900. Check others at the same address and note names of neighbours for possible contact. Some museums keep geneology lists.

4. Try to trace your birth parents through their past. Look for obituaries that name closes relatives such as, "Mr. John Smith is survived by his daughter Rose." Obtain a copy of your grandparents' death certificates from Vital Statistics, and copies of all papers filed with Probate from Surrogate Court. In some provinces this is called Probate Registry to the Supreme Court. In your state you may get your ancestors' names from the State Department of Vital Statistics. This will tell you in what county your ancestor died. Then apply to the County Superior Court for information on Probate.

5. In Canada, write to Public Archives, Geneology Division, 395 Wellington St., Ottawa, Ontario. In the U.S., write to Geneology Department of the Church of Jesus Christ of Latter Day Saints, 50 East N. Temple, Salt Lake City, Utah, 84150. This registry may also be available in your local library or centre for geneology research.

6. Look for church marriage records.

7. Try the voters' lists which may be kept at city hall.

8. Check automobile registrations if that is possible in your province or state.

9. Talk to bill collectors.

10. Try relatives no matter how distant. Pretend you are researching family geneology. The word "adoption" can close off information.

11. If you find a document, try talking to all the people whose names appear on the document, including witnesses or an attending priest or minister.

12. Search for employers that your birth parents may have had.

13. If they were in unionized employment, ask the union to check their records. If they graduated from high school or university,

          check school records. These may give you their former address
          or even a picture.

14   Hospital records. Some hospitals destroy their records. Others
          may need a "waiver of confidentiality" from an adoption agency
          or government department.

15.   Check the newspaper: information wanted, missing persons,
          personal, anniversary, obituaries, marriages.

16.   Check old newspapers for marriages, births, and deaths.

17.   Persevere.

The most useful piece of information searchers can have to begin with is their birth name. A name somehow makes the adoptee and the birth mother more real. If adoptees don't have their name, they need as much other information as they can get. They need to find out where they were born—city, state or province, and hospital; their birth date, weight, and information such as the name of the attending doctor and nurse. Adoptees also need to know the city, state or province in which they were adpoted; what agency placed them and when; and the date the adoption was completed. Sometimes, after a meticulous and systematic search, critical information will arise serendipitously, from a chance meeting or an overheard conversation.

At a meeting of health workers in the area where my youngest son's birth grandparents had lived twenty-five years earlier, I talked to a health nurse from his Native nation who knew everyone in the community. After one brief meeting and an exchange of letters, she and I became the bridge that allowed my son and his birth mother to connect. Serendipity does happen.

With the Internet and other fast communication systems, and with the more open attitude toward adoption, adoptees will find the search much easier than the tedious and difficult paths of the past. Adoptees need to talk to other adoptees about their searches, to support groups and, if at all possible, to their adoptive parents. It is important to be prepared for the feelings that come with either rejection or reunion. Both can be overwhelming.

If searchers have only non-identifying information, they may find something in that information that can be traced. It is necessary to become a detective—questioning, prying, snooping, perhaps even lying a little—to explore each clue, follow every possible loose thread. They may find some indication of what school their birth parents attended, awards they might have won, employment they or their parents might have had. Social workers sometimes get tired of blocking out the names in the non-identifying information near the end of a report. Partially erased names and other half blacked-out words can provide clues.

Some people see the search as an intense emotional journey, others as an intellectual challenge. "With the odds against me, the world against me, I'll win," Barry said. "It's like my theme song is 'Never Surrender'."

Rhea, at seventeen, had searched alone, finding her birth mother by putting together all the information she could. "I knew she had been a teacher, that she was blonde, five-foot-six inches, blue eyes. I didn't know where she lived, but I knew she had grade thirteen in Ontario. I had my last name narrowed down to five names. I found that out by snatching glances at the records as the social workers pulled them out."

Leslie, in her search, had honed her detective skills quite well. "The name of the town my birth mother lived in was on the adoption form. I figured it was a small town and there must be somebody there who knew what was going on. I wrote to the church. The minister might know. He might tell me a lot about her without telling me her name. I didn't have to know who she was. I just needed to know more about her. I thought so, anyway. I wrote to the Children's Aid Society there. They've got two of them. I wrote to the hospital and I wrote to the library checking for birth announcements from that date [Leslie's birthday].

"And what happened was that the lady in the library knew the family, knew that there was another child out there, and she forwarded my letter to one of my sisters who still lived out there. And my sister answered the letter, not letting on for a minute that she knew who I was or that she knew that she was my sister. She just asked me what I wanted to know and I wrote back and told her. I didn't care if they had a million bucks. All I wanted was to know. I wasn't in it for the money.

"And the hospital made the mistake of writing back and telling me. They aren't supposed to disclose that kind of information, but they wrote back and they told me that there was a child born to Mary Smith and she named me after herself. And they made the mistake of telling me. Maybe they didn't realize what they were doing. Or maybe she [birth mother] put it in there that if anyone ever did inquire they were allowed to give it out."

Some teens feared that if they started to search for their birth parents, they might receive an unexpected and unwanted visit from a birth mother or father. It is the policy of searching agencies not to allow unscheduled meetings between parties, but it sometimes happens. Adopted children are supposed to be asked if they want a meeting, but occasionally mistakes are made and a birth mother bypasses an agency and makes direct contact. This is rare, but possible.

Joining a group can give an adoptee a sense of acceptance. The others in the group will see the searcher's needs as reasonable and normal. Others who are experienced searchers may offer advice and help. Most organizations will not actively assist a search for birth parents, but they will provide information and advice on how to deal with difficulties.

While a group of searchers can be a great support, the members of the group are diverse. No one will have identical problems. People with different ideas and different needs join the group, but since they have a common goal, they are usually willing to provide information and understanding.

Each adopted person must decide what it is they need to discover and how important it is to them. Many adopted teens at about fifteen or sixteen are working through feelings of independence and have difficulty with their adoptive parents, particularly mothers. At times they think that all their problems would be solved if they could only meet their birth parents, that they could be magically freed from the task of working things out with their adoptive parents. They imagine that they would be loved and understood, instinctively accepted by "real" parents.

But, of course, there aren't any magical ways of working out a relationship. Relationships take time and effort. Everyone must work at it, adopted or not. Dealing with relationships, solving the problem of parental authority in the move toward independence, are the usual tasks of teen life. This must not be confused with searching for original history in an effort to establish identity.

Teens who are not adopted sometimes "adopt" another set of parents during this turbulent time. They tell their own parents nothing and tell their friends' parents everything. I've often wondered if it wouldn't be wise to trade fifteen-year-olds around the neighbourhood. My child would go to the neighbour's and her kid would come to live at my house. Some teens told me that they stayed with aunts or neighbours for a while, so perhaps to some extent, this is already happening.

Most searching agencies understand this painful growing period and will advise teens to wait until they are eighteen. By then, they will have resolved most of their problems of independence, and some of the problems of identity, and will be ready and strong enough to take on new relationships.

Debbie told me very firmly, "I'm sixteen. I have a set of parents [adoptive]. I have foster parents, a sister, and two brothers. I have a foster sister and brother, a boy friend, school, and a job. I don't have *time* for any more relationships."

Not all teens wanted to search for their beginnings. Some just wanted to talk to someone about it, to work out their feelings, get their ideas clear. Professional counsellors may be helpful: school counsellors, ministers, social workers. A friendly aunt or uncle, an older brother or sister—sometimes a neighbour might be easy to talk to, listen well, and give good advice Sometimes all that is needed to assuage the curiosity teens have about their past is to talk about it.

How many parents do adopted children have? Most teens only wanted to know who their birth parents were and perhaps meet them, not move them into a parental position. They already had parents who filled the mother and father spots in their hearts and they didn't want those parents moved—even slightly—from that central position.

"I don't want another mother," Sue-ann said. "She [her adoptive mother] doesn't understand about my wanting to search, but she loves me. I don't doubt it for a moment and I don't want to hurt her."

Some teens had concerns that, if they searched for birth parents, they might be abandoned by their adoptive parents the way they had been abandoned at birth. No matter how people talked about "relinquishment," "giving up," "making a birth plan," and "placing you in a loving home," some teens still felt they had been abandoned. They didn't want to risk that again.

Teens often dealt with these feelings successfully by organizing their lives so that they knew where their parents and loved ones were at all times and what to expect day by day. They were reassured by the consistent patterns and predictable reliability of their loved ones.

Some adoptive parents are casual and think teens should be able to adjust to changes in plans and unexpected revisions in time schedules. "I can't *always* be on time," they say. Such parents think detailed planning is too rigid, and too difficult to follow. "Lighten up," they say. Adopted teens might find this attitude very hard to live with.

Parents may need to understand the importance of predictability and control in their adopted child's life. If teens find loss and rejection almost overwhelming, a predictable time schedule helps. At some time in their lives, they will have to deal with the need for regulation and consistency, which is due to fears of abandonment, but their feelings are not unusual. Many people create rigid schedules and a predictable lifestyle for themselves. It is a coping mechanism that often works.

If adoptive parents divorce, teens may feel the loss of a parent even more deeply than a teen who has not been adopted. At that time the emotions of abandonment at birth may resurface as well as the rational concerns of all teens such as: "Will I ever see Dad again?" (Or Mom, if it is the mother who has left the house.) "Will I be able to call him?" "Will I still be his kid?"

Teens have friends with divorced parents where one of those parents stops calling and visiting with the child—where the parent simply disengages. The threat of that kind of loss could cause emotional panic in the adopted teen.

At the time of a divorce or when teens fear abandonment, it helps them to talk to someone, preferably someone from an adoption agency such as Adoptive Families Association, who will understand their strong concerns about losing a parent. If the teen is from an distinctive ethnic culture, he or she might find a counsellor at their cultural centre, such as a First Nations Healing Centre or an Indian Friendship Centre.

Divorce is a loss in the life of a teen, and while loss and abandonment are often difficult for adopted teens, life is full of loss. It is part of the human condition to love and lose. Adopted teens will, in time, learn how to deal with the losses of their lives. It usually helps enormously to deal with the first loss, to get an explanation of why they were relinquished for adoption and connect with their birth mother. This meeting, this reunion, makes their past concrete and so makes them feel more real. They had been dancing on shifting sand for years, and want to stomp their feet on firm ground, shouting, "This is *my* part of the world. These are *my* roots. This is *my* mother."

Those feelings don't match their intellectual appraisal of the situation. This birth mother is their mother—sort of. This birth family is their family—sort of. Intellectually they can slot their birth parents into the past, but emotionally they need them in the present.

Finding a birth mother is not like meeting an aunt or a cousin who had been away for years. Meeting a birth mother is like meeting yourself, a kind of doppelganger, a self-ghost. It can be shocking and very disturbing. It touches at the pit of anger and depression buried deep within. If the birth mother is friendly and supportive, teens may still hate her for giving them up: "Why me?" "What was wrong with me?" The mind knows that she was eighteen, poor, possibly in an abusive home, and that for the child's safety and a better future, she gave it to adoptive parents. But the heart doesn't always take direction from the mind, and teens may feel betrayed, angry, and confused.

If teens understand that their feelings of loss may have come from their first separation from their birth mother, they must acknowledge that powerful feelings are at work inside them and not underestimate the effects of a reunion. Teens may decide that they are not emotionally ready to deal with a reunion with their birth mother. If they are trying to cope with an addiction, another big loss in their life, or an abusive relationship, they may need to leave the task of reunion to another time.

As in the other areas of life, if teens explain to those who love them what their fears and concerns are and let them know what help they need, they are far more likely to get it than if they act out their feelings in anger or a self-destructive lifestyle. Most parents aren't psychologists; they are more likely to respond to their teen's actions rather than their feelings unless teens find a way to tell their parents why they are upset. A counsellor can help make this clear to parents.

If teens find their birth mother and are rejected, their emotional responses are more than doubled. The feelings of rejection are compounded. They must realize that it wasn't their fault that their mother couldn't keep them at birth, and it isn't their fault she can't accept them now. She is probably dealing with problems in her own life that make it hard for her to accept *any* child at this time. Still, rejection, for any reason, is extremely difficult to take.

Birth mothers find themselves in an emotional situation where there are few roadmaps or protocols for behaviour. The reunion is a situation without guidelines for the adopted child and the adoptive parents. As well as reading books written about the process, counselling can be very useful at this time, helping everyone to cope with the ramifications of the meeting.

Once teens find their birth parents, how do they fit them into their lives? This depends on their present family situation, on the feelings their birth mother (or father) has for them, and on their experience with their adoptive parents. If their parents are divorced, they may have a stepmother and already have experience with several mothers or fathers.

I remember walking through the village of Arctic Bay in Northern Baffin Island and being introduced to an old woman by my friend, Meena, who said, "This is my grandmother." After we left the woman, Meena said, "You understand that I have many grandmothers who are not related by birth?" Any woman who loved her was a "grandmother." Teens may have grandmothers and mothers of affection in their lives and know how to make room for many kinds of relationships. There are many different ways of incorporating people into their lives; they need to think about how they can make room for their birth mother. If teens have grown up in an open adoption where they have always known their birth mother, including her will likely not be a problem.

When adopted teens meet their birth mother or talk to her on the phone for the first time, it's a good idea for them to take time to think about the encounter before they meet again. "Take it slow" is the best advice. Teens need time to adjust, and birth mothers do as well.

Teens want to feel in control of whether they meet and how often; they need to feel in charge of the meetings. They want to be very sure they can retreat from the involvement with their birth mother if they find it too stressful.

Rachelle had known her birth mother for six years and her birth father for two. At the café where I met her for lunch, she told me that she had numerous parents, but none of them willing to accept her. She had an adoptive mother, an adoptive father, an Aunt Louise, a birth mother, a birth father, a best girlfriend, and her girlfriend's family. As well, she had to cope with social workers and her employer. Her relationships were intricate and complicated.

Her birth mother, Suzanne, was not a stranger to her family. She was the sister of Rachelle's adoptive mother.

Her adoptive mother Ella, sister to her birth mother Suzanne, does not have a simple, straight-forward family. She divorced Rachelle's adoptive father and married Jose. Jose, now Rachelle's stepfather, molested Rachelle, so she left to go live with her mother's other sister, her Aunt Louise, and her cousin Annie. Her adoptive mother was pregnant at this time. The baby will not have a simple relationship to Rachelle either, for she will be Rachelle's legal sister, but also her cousin.

Her Aunt Louise took Rachelle in and supported her. Her aunt's home was a stable one and Rachelle felt accepted there, but her birth mother Suzanne wanted Rachelle with her, was "jealous," Rachelle says, and so she went to her birth mother's house. Rachelle had almost too many mothers.

Rachelle's birth mother was an alcoholic and a drug user and while emotional about Rachelle, she had not been supportive. Rachelle stayed with her birth mother for a few months, but the drug parties and lack of structure and food made it hard. Her mother kicked her out and told her not to go to any of the family. She told her sisters she was practising "tough love" on Rachelle, and not to take her in. This meant that, even with three mothers, she had no place to go.

Her birth father, John, was introduced to her when she was thirteen by her Aunt Louise. John was simply her birth father and not related to her in any other way. He had a wife and three children. His wife did not want Rachelle in her family. Her birth father was willing to give Rachelle money occasionally, but could not give her a home with his family.

Rachelle had an adoptive father who had left the family, a stepfather who had abused her, and a biological father who lived apart from her. She had almost too many fathers, with none taking responsibility for her.

Rachelle called a social worker in December and told her that she had been kicked out by her mother and had no place to stay. The welfare agency said they'd call her back. She phoned several times without getting any help. It was now March, three months later, and they had never called her or concerned themselves with where she was living.

At fifteen, Rachelle found a couple who needed a nanny for their baby. In return for babysitting they gave her a home and food. She had enrolled in high school correspondence courses and worked on them while she was child minding. She was doing well and plans to graduate with her class.

Knowing their birth mother does not necessarily create magical, supportive families for teens, as Rachelle's life attests. It helps to know her background, but she doesn't look for mothering from Suzanne. With four parents, three stepparents, an aunt, an adult friend, and the social agencies, Rachelle, at fifteen, had no one who took responsibility for her, although she had found some positive, supporting adults in her life. Her Aunt Louise and her cousin had managed to evade the family directive and gave her unconditional love and support. She had, she said, talked about her feelings and expectations of all her parents, and has dealt with her anger about her life. Her family relationships are complicated and difficult, but she is determined to make a good life for herself, and she will manage.

Rachelle was an amazing young woman who had worked through many of her issues around loss and rejection as she struggled for her own place in the world. Meeting her birth father was very important to her. He was a stable, reliable man in his own second family and, although he couldn't bring Rachelle into that family, he maintained contact and gave her some financial support as her right as one of his children.

Once teens know who their birth father is, they need to decide whether they want contact with him. If they resent him for leaving their birth mother without support, they may feel too angry to meet him. If they think that, "Hey, they were both young and in trouble," and can understand that, they might contact him. It may be that their conception was the result of rape or incest. That situation is very difficult for children to accept, and they will need to talk it over with a trusted adult. But once teens have worked through their hurt and anger in what is often a complicated process, there is no reason why they can't be successful and happy.

Teens need to decide what they want to know from their birth parents. Usually two or three meetings are necessary before they feel comfortable enough to ask why they were given up, what their medical history is, and who the other family members are.

Sometimes there are family members who didn't know about the teen's birth. The sudden appearance of a sixteen-year-old might come as a big surprise. There may be a warm response from the biological brothers and sisters. Uncles may call and invite them to family celebrations. Grandparents may ask for a visit. Teens need to decide how much contact they want with birth family members. If they are lucky, their problem will be one of deciding who to visit first.

If they are not so lucky, they may find that the relatives of their birth parents don't want to know them and aren't interested in seeing them. Teens may be limited to getting information from their birth parents with no contact at all with other relatives. This might be difficult to accept. It's unlikely that the family took one look at the teen and said, "We don't want anything to do with that one!" and more likely that there are current social and family problems that the appearance of the teen would complicate.

When teens look for their birth parents, their adoptive parents may not be supportive. In spite of all that has been written about the importance of adoptive parents helping their children to search for their birth parents, and about how helping adopted children search will bring them closer to adoptive parents, many are still afraid of the search. In fact, teens *very* often told me that their adoptive parents would be hurt by their search. Their parents would think, they said, that they wanted another set of parents. It is sometimes true that adoptive parents feel threatened by a child's possible reunion with the birth family.

Although not specifically stated, the fear that in the search for their birth parents they might risk losing the warm, supportive relationship they had with their adoptive parents might have been an underlying concern. Teens need to be clear about whether their adoptive parents really will be hurt and afraid of a search, or whether it is they themselves who are afraid.

I believe that all adoptive children should know their birth parents—at least their names, where they live, and what they do in their lives—and that adoptive parents should help their children find this information. That doesn't mean that teens should immediately start their search.

There may be good reasons not to search. Teens may believe it wiser to wait for a few years when they can search without involving their adoptive parents. They know their adoptive parents better than anyone else. A compulsion to search for a birth mother and the information she can give is perfectly normal and natural and usually doesn't threaten the relationship with adoptive parents, but perhaps the adoptive parent would be hurt and the teen knows this. An adopted child may eventually find the right time, when searching may be easier, and the energy to do so.

It is my hope that adopted teens realize that the uncertain feelings they have—that they are aliens on this planet, different, don't quite belong, will be abandoned without support—have been created by a system that takes a child from one mother and gives it to another while prohibiting contact between the mothers, and not because of any lack in the teens. Adopted teens have adjusted in the best way they could, responding like any normal, healthy baby or child would.

Our society, including everyone involved in the adoption process, but especially the teens themselves, needs to recognize and accept these feelings as normal in the circumstances. The effects of adoption begin before birth and last throughout life. Adopted teens must work to prevent the fears and uncertainties about their adoption from overpowering their lives.

Afterword

I MET OVER FIFTY TEENS WHILE I was researching this book. Many people who were not teens and who heard I was writing a book about adoption called to talk to me. A birth father wanted to know if I had talked to his daughter because he was looking for her; birth mothers wanted me to tell their children how they felt; foster children, adoptive parents, adopted adults, and more teenagers than I could possibly find the time to see called. Teens whom I had interviewed years ago called to tell me what was going on in their lives. Teens whom I had only recently interviewed called to ask me if I was *still* working on the book and wanted to know when it would be published. Everyone had a particular interest in some aspect of adoption.

I asked teens twenty-nine questions that covered many topics. Sometimes they stayed within the subject of the questions; sometimes the questions were a stimulus for long conversations about their present life, their past, and their expectations.

I couldn't predict how they would answer all the questions I asked, but after about ten interviews, I was quite sure how they would answer at least some of them. The teens had many feelings and ideas that they had arrived at independently, but which they held in common.

Most importantly, they wanted to know their original names, why they were given up for adoption, and their general social and medical histories. They wanted to either meet their birth mother or see her, and to be in control of any meeting with birth parents. They didn't want birth parents to take the place of their adoptive parents; they just wanted knowledge of their beginnings.

141

Teens usually didn't know how to search for information, even where to start or whom to call first. They had vague ideas that somewhere there would be an accurate record or their birth and original name: in a hospital, in a welfare office, in a lawyer's office. Most thought social welfare offices held their personal background information in secret, and resented the system that refused to give them this information. They looked on their need to know about their birth as personal and private, and generally hadn't thought much about the fact that there are many teenagers with similar needs. And they didn't see themselves as having the power to make changes in the system.

They did not think that being adopted in any way restricted their social opportunities; they didn't feel any social prejudice against adoption even when adoption was transracial. The fact that they were adopted would not in any way restrict their employment, social opportunities, or family life. They would adopt children themselves.

In other ways they were all different in their need for information, emotional responses to families and friends, and degrees of independence, ambition, and ability. Some had few concerns about the process of adoption; others had many. Some poured out their feelings about the problems society caused them; others couldn't see what the drama was all about. All were interesting, informative, and eager to share their ideas. They were especially eager to share with other teenagers who have thought their thoughts, lived with their worries, and shared their feelings.

Adopted teenagers contribute significantly to changes in attitude toward adoption because the social atmosphere that affects the next generation is established by what we do today. The first step toward positive change is to help teens understand themselves, to become more aware of what they think and why. Perhaps this book will help teens toward reaching the goal of knowing how they feel, and what they want and need.

As well, the voices of the teens in this book will help parents and care workers to better understand what adoption looks like from the teen's point of view. With that information, parents and care workers will be better able to help construct a world in which adoption is a positive and sustaining aspect of teen life—a process of creating a unique and emotionally fulfilling family.

Throughout this book I have spoken of adoption generally, as if adoption occurred at infancy and the child went into a home with two parents. While this was true for the teens I interviewed, there are, of course, many other adoption stories. Adoptions occur at all ages of a person's life and can happen even in adulthood. Stepparents adopt their partner's children, aunts and uncles adopt. Single people adopt and same-sex couples adopt. These are seldom mentioned or given positions in reports, books and on TV, but they are important. A great deal of what the teens had to say to me will apply to the children in those adoption stories as well. I recognize the diversity of adoption families and I hope that the teens' stories here will be useful to teens whatever their adoption experience.

The experience of adoption continually changes. Adoptive parents can now wait as long as ten years for a child. Adoptive parents are taking more initiative in finding an agency, contracting a home study, financially supporting a birth mother through pregnancy and delivery, and adapting to continually new and challenging changes in society's attitudes about adoption. Private agencies are now available to help parents look for children and to help birth parents place their child, as are books which can help guide adopting parents through the process of finding a child. While there is interesting research on fertilization techniques to help couples who have great difficulty conceiving a biological child, the techniques are still, for the most part, abysmally unsuccessful, as well as time-consuming, financially draining, and emotionally painful. Adoption is still a possible and positive experience for many.

The ways in which we look for a child to adopt, look for parents to adopt a child, and look for information at all stages of the process, will continue to change as social attitudes and technology change. The concerns around secrecy and open adoption continue to evolve as well.

With the increasing necessity for identifying numbers—social insurance numbers, employment numbers, registration numbers in schools and universities—individuals will find their lives tabulated and stored as information in many different places. With the increasing developments in technological access to information, the facts about our existence are recorded more and more often.

It still comes as a surprise to me that when I type my name on an Internet search I find myself—name, picture, list of books. That experience will become more common, I believe, as technology invents more ways to disseminate information. Everyone will be able to type in their name and find their life achievements (and possibly credit problems) listed on a Web site. With this ability to find information will come new challenges. A birth mother could transfer her picture to a Web site with pertinent information about where and when she had given up her child. A searching child who only has to be old enough to know how to search could contact that mother. This makes efforts at secrecy seem inadequate and useless. In the future we will have to deal with issues around adoption and connecting with birth parents much earlier in a child's life than in the past.

Conversely, an adopted child could put her information on line and a birth mother or other relative could easily find her. This process is open to anyone, including parasites who leech onto the hopes and fantasies of unconnected adopted children hoping to make money from them, or behave in other unsavoury and predatory ways. Still, for children who were never told or who don't know who their birth mothers are, the Internet will be an efficient and affordable way to find their background.

Adoption agencies that continue to try to hide identifying information about birth parents will find it more and more difficult as our society becomes technologically adept. In North America today, adoptive families currently looking for birth parents find the process much easier than it was even fifteen years ago. Data is available on a Net search that would have taken years and much travel to find in the past. Of course, in less technologically sophisticated countries it is more difficult to find information. Families who adopted from less-developed countries where there is no central data or registration office that can send information via e-mail may hit stonewalling, blocks to information, lack of access, and no information at all. "The orphanage burned down" can be a dead end for a searching adopted child or family in a country where there is no central data storage. Storing information in data banks ensures that all the orphanages can burn down and the information will still be available. Countries where central data banks are not available will probably have them in the near future.

Travelling is easier now and may be even more so in the future, so families will find international adoption an increasingly attractive option. More parents will adopt children of races different from their own. This may be only slightly ahead of changes in the mosaic of the common culture.

Increasing interaction between cultures and more immigration of diverse races will result in more intermarriages. With intermarriage comes cultural acceptance—if you don't accept your daughter-in-law, you don't get to see your grandchildren. These marriages will produce racially diverse children and families, which will become more common until they are obvious and accepted in mainstream society. Interracially adopted families will then blend into the new society, and find themselves less of a curiosity in the grocery line-up.

With increasing opportunities to travel, families who have adopted internationally may find it easier to visit the country of their child's origin and become familiar with the culture. The child's experience of being part of the majority while the adoptive parents are the minority can be emotionally insightful for both the adopted child and the adoptive parents. Parents will understand their child's world view much better. As well, it is very difficult for parents to accurately convey the culture of their adopted child if they have few friends and little contact from that culture. A trip to the country of the children's origins will at least show them that there is a valuable and well-established world that will accept them *because* of their appearance.

Adoptive families need to learn how to create strong bonds of love and loyalty, the way all families need to know how to create such bonds. They must do this in a North American culture which continually tests family bonds with divorce and remarriage. Children today, from biological and adoptive families, are experiencing the disruptive change of divorcing parents and will continue to do so. Families need to become more aware of the diverse nature of "family." What is it that unifies a family, makes it whole? What can be done to maintain family strength and loyalty? The concept of a family, biological or adoptive, must survive difficult times—such as when a parent leaves the family and begins or joins another one—which threatens the very idea of its unity. Socially and personally, families need to be committed to a sense of what family means, and adoptive families need to be even more conscious of what they believe a family should be, and what their commitment is to it. They may have to decide what it is about their family that is important and how they can maintain and sustain it.

Our North American formal education rarely teaches us how to be emotionally mature and wise. Maturity and wisdom which come with experience are necessary in being a good parent, being happily adopted, and being able to engage in intimate and sustaining relationships. I have, over the past thirty years, been grateful to my adopted sons, my stepdaughter and my biological daughter for the joys and lessons they have brought to my life and to their contributions to my sense of family.

Resources

The Library

There are many books on the subject of adoption, but be sure to look at the date of publication. Adoption laws have changed a great deal in the past ten years, so sources that tell you how to search should be recently published. Sources that talk about how adoptees feel can be published years ago and still be useful.

A list of books that might be helpful are contained in the bibliography at the back of this book. Check the backs of other books where relevant books are listed. Some organizations such as the Adoptive Families Association have a library of recommended books that you can borrow.

Adoption Organizations

Check your area and decide which ones might answer your questions. They have names such as: Adoptive Families Association (a good place for adoptees to find information as well), Parent Finders, Adoption Support Group, Adoptive Families of Native Children, First Nations Reunification (for First Nations adoptees looking for birth families). Phone and ask about the organization's purpose, meeting times, and who attends. Look for an adoptee support group, or an Adoptive Parents Association for both adoptees and adoptive parents.

Newsletters

Many organizations put out regular newsletters. You can get a list of the newsletters from the library and from the Internet.

The Internet
Some libraries allow time on their computers to browse the Internet, where you can find recent information and sometimes birth parents. Canadopt and various U.S. Web sites offer names of birth mothers and family members if they are looking for you. Remember to take the information, but don't respond immediately. Talk about your feelings and plans with a trusted adult who can help counsel you before you take the next step to contact that name. Be prepared for the disappointment if the name you contact is not the person you seek, of, if it is, be prepared for the possibility of rejection.

The following are some addresses that you can check. Internet addresses change quickly, so you may need to search "adoptee search" or "adoption" to find new or different sources. Don't put your name and address on the Internet unless you are prepared for weird, strange, even unscrupulous contacts. Internet addresses change each day so these addresses may have disappeared. You will find others, though, and some can be useful.

> *www.webreflection.com/aiml/uslaws.html*
> laws concerning adoption records in the U.S.
> *www.nebula.on.ca/canadopt*
> offers a path to many informative sites
> *www.psy.ucsd.edu/~jhartung/adopt.inf*
> how to search
> *www.psy.ucsd.edu/~jhartung/open.html*
> U.S. and Canada legislation on open records
> *www.psy.ucsd.edu/~jhartung/canada.txt*
> organizations in Canada—with many interesting and useful links
> *www.members.aol.com/TRIAD2271/index.html*
> excellent site with advice and hints on how to search
> *www.absnw.com/reunions/bookstore/*
> provides information on books

Bibliography

Aigner, Hal. *Faint Trails: A Guide to Adult Adoptee-Birth Parent Reunification Searches.* Greenbrace, CA: Paradigm Press, 1987.

Ames, Elinor. "Psychological Studies on Adoption." *British Columbia Medical Journal* 26. March No 3 (1984).

Bascom, Barbara B., and Carole A. McKelvey. *The Complete Guide to Foreign Adoption: What to Expect, and How to Prepare for Your New Child.* New York: Pocket Books, 1997.

Bean, Philp, and Joy Melville. *Lost Children of the Empire.* London, Sydney, Wellington: Unwin Hyman, 1989.

Bothun, Linda. *Dialogues about Adoption: Conversations between Parents and Their Children.* Chey Chase, Maryland: Swan Publications, 1994.

Boult, B.E. "Suicide attempts among adolescent adoptees." *South African Medical Journal* 74. September (1988).

Caplan, Lincoln. *An Open Adoption.* New York: Fararr, Straus & Giroux, 1990.

Carp, E. Wayne. *Family Matters: Secrecy and Disclosure in the History of Adoption.* Cambridge, MA: Harvard University Press, 1998.

Coyle, Stephen B. Smart and Michael. *Aboriginal Issues Today: A Legal and Business Guide.* North Vancouver: Self Counsel Press, 1997.

Crook, Marion. *Suicide: Teens Talk to Teens.* North Vancouver: Self Council Press, 1997.

Daly, Kerry J., and Michael P. Sobol. "Adoption in Canada." Guelph, ON: National Adoption Study, University of Guelph, 1993. 167.

Dorris, Michael. *The Broken Chord.* New York: Harper Collins, 1990.

Fahlberg, Vera I. *A Child's Journey through Placement.* Indianapolis: Perspective Press, 1991.

Gabel, Susan. *Filling in the Blanks: A Guided Look at Growing Up Adopted.* Indianapolis, Indiana: Perspective Press.

Gritten, James C. *Adoption without Fear.* San Antonio: Corona Publishing, 1989.

Groza, Victor, and Karen R. Rosenberg. *Clinical and Practice Issues in Adoption: Bridging the Gap between Adoptees Placed as Infants and as Older Children.* Westport, Connecticut, London: Praeger, 1998.

Holden, Neil L. "Adoption and eating disorders: a high-risk group?" *Journal of Psychiatry* 158. June (1991): 829-833.

Howe, David. *Patterns of Adoption: Nature, Nurture a Psychosocial Development. Working Together for Children, Young People and Their Families.* Ed. Olive Stevenson. Oxford: Blackwell Science, 1998.

Jacobs, Wendy. "Adoption and suicide in Australia." *Suicide Prevention: the Global Context.* Eds. R.J. Kosky, et al. New York: Plenum Publishers, 1998.

Kety, Seymour S. "Genetic factors in suicide: family, twin, and adoption studies." *Suicide Over the Life Cycle: Risk Factors, Assessment and Treatment of Suicidal Patients.* Eds. S. J. Bluemnthal and D.J. Kupfer. Washington DC: American Psychiatric Press, 1990.

Kirk, David H. *Adoptive Kinship: A Modern Institution in Need of Reform.* Port Angeles: Ben-Simon Publishers, 1981, 1985.

Kirk, David H. *Exploring Adoptive Family Life: The Collected Papers.* Port Angeles: Ben-Simon Publishers, 1988.

Kirk, David H. *Shared Fate.* Brentwood Bay: Ben-Simon Publications, 1964, 1984.

March, Karen. *The Stranger Who Bore Me: Adoptee-Birth Mother Relationships.* Toronto: University of Toronto Press, 1995.

Melina, Lois Rusakai. *Making Sense of Adoption: A Parent's Guide.* New York: Harper & Row, 1989.

Melina, Lois Rusakai. *The Open Adoption Experience.* New York: Harper Perennial, 1993.

Monserrat, Jeanne Linsay and Catherine. *Adoption Awareness: A Guide for Teachers, Counselors, Nurses and Caring Others.* Buena Park: Morning Glory Press, 1989.

Pierce, Christine Adamec and William L. *The Encyclopedia of Adoption.* New York: Facts on File, 1991.

Pinar, William. "Seminar, University of British Columbia," 1999.

Robinson, Evelyn. Adoption as a risk factor in youth suicide." *Suicide Prevention; The Global Context.* Eds. R.J. Kosky, et al. New York: Plenum Publishers, 1998.

Takas, Marianne, and Edward Warner. *To Love a Child: A Complete Guide to Adoption, Foster Parenting, and Other Ways to Share Your Life with*

Children. Reading, MA: Addison-Wesley Publishing Company, 1992.

Taney, Richard F. Ramsay and Bryan L. *Global Trends in Suicide Prevention: Toward the Development of National Strategies for Suicide Prevention.* Mumbai, Indian: Tata Institute of Social Sciences, 1996.

Verrier, Nancy Newton. *The Primal Wound: Understanding the Adopted Child.* Baltimore, MD: Gateway Press Inc., 1993,1996.

Ward, Margaret. *The Adoption of Native Canadian Children.* Cobalt, ON: Highway Book Shop, 1984.

Wegar, Katarina. *Adoption, Identity and Kinship: The Debate over Sealed Birth Records.* New Haven, London: Yale University Press, 1997.

Wine, Judith. *The Canadian Adoption Guide.* Toronto, Montreal: McGraw-Hill Ryerson, 1995.